Time for Transition

by

Dr. Robert A. Enos

Time for Transition

by

Dr. Robert A. Enos

www.gwcclancaster.org

Time for Transition

Requests for bulk sales discounts, editorial permissions, or other information should be addressed to:

Additional copies available at:

www.gwcclancaster.org
gwccrobert@gmail.com
+1-661-942-7000

Trade Paperback ISBN: 978-1-387-16989-4
eBook ISBN: 978-1-387-16994-8

Cover Design by Darian Horner Design (www.darianhorner.com)

Printed in the United States of America

10 9 8 7 6 5 4 3 2 1

Contents

Acknowledgements

The two most important people I want to say Thank You to is my wife, Linda and to Jesus, my best friend. Linda, you encouraged me every step of the way. You truly are an amazing woman. Jesus, my Savior and Friend. You are my everything. I'm lost without You. I pray that You are pleased with this book.

Dr. Ron and Adina Horner, I appreciate all you've done to make this book a reality. You made me look much smarter than I am, and that is hard work. Thank you.

A special thanks to the Greater Works Christian Church family for putting up with me the way you do. You got to hear me preach this long before it was a book and you didn't run away screaming. GWCC, you are the best!

I also want to show my love for my children and grandbabies. When I look at you I know I must do whatever I can to make the world a better place for you and your generations. I love and appreciate you more than you will ever know.

I want to say, thank you to everyone that has made a positive impact on my life. This book is a product of your influence and friendship in my life.

Foreword

Transition can be one of the most difficult times of life, but we can't escape its reality. Whether good or bad, transition is common to man. Rob Enos offers a fresh perspective on transition with prophetic insight and practical teaching on how to embrace change and transition well to the next assignment God has ordained for you. If you are walking through transition now and are feeling disoriented and discouraged, you need to read this book! It's a breath of fresh air to those contending for God's "next" in their lives.

Jennifer LeClaire
Former editor, *Charisma* magazine
Senior Leader, *Awakening House of Prayer*
Founder, *Ignite Network*

IV

Introduction

Over the years I have received several prophecies telling me to write a book. It wasn't just one prophet, but numerous prophets and prophetic people that spoke these words to me. Even though these words kept piling up, I didn't set aside the time and make writing a book a priority. Well, I finally made time and wrote this book.

I decided to not only write about what burned in my heart for the church, but what I feel is extremely important for the times we are in. As this book discusses, we are in major transition and change in the world and the church. As much as we like the security of things that rarely change, or are slow to change, this type of security is hard to find today. Since this is the case, we the church must learn to change as well. We must learn how to navigate the changes that are upon us by changing with them. It would be beneficial to us all if we could recognize that changes that are upon us and be wise enough to direct those changes to match the will of God. In doing so we could drive these transitions in such a way that it benefits us all.

Transition can be defined as: a change from one way of living and existing to another. This is exactly what we in the church today are experiencing. Our very existence is shifting and changing into something we're not fully aware of yet. What we look like today is not what we will look like 10 years from now. The transitions are here whether we want them or not. When we recognize the change that is taking place we can rise up and be the ones that take the change where God wants it taken. If we don't take our rightful place at the helm of these transition then someone else will. The changes upon us may be directed by the wicked if the righteous will not rise up and make the changes as we should.

In this book, I attempted to take a hard, but honest look at the condition of the church today. Doing this means that we will be facing some problems that need to be addressed. It is not my intention to merely point out problems, but to provide answers to the problems that are addressed. Here you will face some of the problems in the church today, but you will also find solutions to these problems.

In the medical field, many are beginning to acknowledge that a more holistic approach to medicine and health is needed. I see that the problems in the church today need a holistic approach in solving these problems, as well. Everything at our disposal should be utilized, especially those things we can only obtain from God. No longer will clever marketing, or mere psychology work at solving spiritual problems. We cannot leave out natural answers, but we must have the deeper answers that only God can give.

As you read this book you will at some point read about yourself. This book is not only about some characters in the Bible, but it is about you. You are the reason I wrote this book. It will help you to know who you are, and where you are in regard to your relationship to God and the church. You will be able to identify some areas that you are strong in, and some areas you need to grow in. God has created each of us to be and do something very special. As you identify some areas you need to make personal changes in you will become more fully the person that God made you to be.

Get ready to be challenged by this book. A friend of mine read the rough draft then called it "Salty." I wasn't exactly sure what he was trying to tell me until I found that salty means, rude, surprising or upsetting. I hope he was saying that this book is surprising and not rude or upsetting. Challenging is the word I would use to describe my book. Challenging to the present system, and challenging to our position in the system, however, I wouldn't write a book pointing out problems in the church unless I also offered answers for those problems.

Please read this book prayerfully and with an open heart. Allow the Holy Spirit to minister to you and reveal what He is saying. God wants you to grow and rise to a much higher level in Him. We are to be more tomorrow than we are today. I believe this book can help.

VIII

Chapter 1
Do We Need Prophets?

Anyone that has been watching world events knows that the world is in a major transition right now. It seems as if the world is coming apart at the seams and hell is winning the battle for the earth. No matter where you turn strange and bad news is being reported from every corner of the globe. Regardless of where we look, it seems as if all stability is gone and chaos is the new norm. As disheartening as this may be for most, this is the atmosphere that God thrives in. This is the type of situation that the Holy Spirit looks for to prove Himself strong.

Genesis 1:1-3

> *[1] In the beginning God created the heavens and the earth.*
>
> *[2] The earth was without form, and void; and darkness was on the face of the deep. And the Spirit of God was hovering over the face of the waters.*
>
> *[3] Then God said, "Let there be light"; and there was light.*

No chaos exists that God cannot handle. No "void" or "darkness" exists that the Holy Spirit cannot fill and illuminate. God thrives in an atmosphere of chaos and an environment that is void and full of darkness. It is here that the Holy Spirit will work to bring light and life out of the darkness, chaos, and emptiness that is all around.

Just as it was at the initial point of creation, it is the same today – nothing overtakes, overwhelms, or catches God off-guard. The same God of Genesis 1 can speak into the darkness of our age and bring forth light. He can talk to our chaos and bring forth order and can speak to the void and emptiness of this generation and bring forth substance and value. Remember this as you look at the chaos in the present world system.

Bear in mind that our God is bigger,
He is greater and more powerful than any evil or
problem in the world today.

One word from our God will turn the whole situation around because the Holy Spirit is now hovering over the chaos of this present age.

The nations of the earth are aligning themselves for a move of God, and they do not even realize it.

The church is being aligned for a move of God
and most in the church do not realize it.

The reason we see such tremendous change in the earth is that something profound is taking place in the spirit realm. We are transitioning from the "Church-Age" to the "Kingdom-Age." We are moving from the standpoint of establishing an assembly and witness in a territory to dominating and completely occupying a territory. Awesome things are being stirred up and are changing even as we speak. Just as in Genesis 1:3, God is about to release a word into our darkness, and our darkness is about to explode into light.

Recently, Apostle Riaan De Lange, from South Africa, was with us and he spoke and prophesied about the transition from Saul to David. This is the transition from the Saul-like kingdom and mentality that has permeated the present church age to the David-like kingdom and mentality of the next phase in church history. The Apostle's message was very timely, but if we do not go back a bit further, to the story of the transition from Eli to Samuel, we will not have the complete understanding of why this is so important. The change from King Saul to King David was not the first transition during this time that impacted Israel and her destiny. A change in the spiritual leadership of the nation occurred before a transition in the political leadership of the country happened. The shift from King Saul to King David gives us clues as to the changes we will face today. In a similar manner, the change from Eli to Samuel also gives us a picture of what is taking place in the realm of the Spirit that will manifest in the natural realm as well.

The story of the transition from Eli to Samuel is important to understand so that we can know how to position ourselves for the transitions that are upon us now. The things that the nation of Israel faced while under the spiritual leadership of Eli and his sons mirror the things we are experiencing today. Just as God transitioned Eli and his sons out to make way for Samuel and his ministry, we are seeing the same types of changes today.

Eli was the High Priest and Judge of Israel when Samuel was born. He was a very well-known and respected religious and political leader of Israel. Although it appears that Eli began his ministry and leadership correctly and in righteousness, he certainly did not end that way. Many of the problems and issues

3

related to Eli and his ministry as High Priest are some of the same things we see today in the modern church.

The Sons of Eli

1 Samuel 2:12-17

¹² *Now the sons of Eli were corrupt; they did not know the LORD.*

¹³ *And the priests' custom with the people was that when any man offered a sacrifice, the priest's servant would come with a three-pronged fleshhook in his hand while the meat was boiling.*

¹⁴ *Then he would thrust it into the pan, or kettle, or caldron, or pot; and the priest would take for himself all that the fleshhook brought up. So they did in Shiloh to all the Israelites who came there.*

¹⁵ *Also, before they burned the fat, the priest's servant would come and say to the man who sacrificed, "Give meat for roasting to the priest, for he will not take boiled meat from you, but raw."*

¹⁶ *And if the man said to him, "They should really burn the fat first; then you may take as much as your heart desires," he would then answer him, "No, but you must give it now; and if not, I will take it by force."*

¹⁷ *Therefore the sin of the young men was very great before the LORD, for men abhorred the offering of the LORD.*

Eli's sons, Hophni and Phinehas, served as priests under their father. As we can see from this passage, they were wicked in what they did as priests. Keep in mind that the priests were to be the ones that modeled holiness and righteousness before the people. They were to teach and lead the people into right relationship with God by modeling their religious beliefs and by teaching the word of God. Their lives were to be a display of right standing with God.

1 Samuel 2:.17

> *"Therefore the sin of the young men was very great before the LORD, for men abhorred the offering of the LORD."*

The priests were to cause the people to rejoice in the Law and the offerings. Hophni and Phinehas caused the people to "abhor the offerings of the Lord." The sons of Eli were so wicked that the people they were to be serving wanted nothing to do with the sacrifices that God required. The people of Israel no longer wanted to offer the very things that kept them free from bondage and sin, and that kept the blessings flowing in their life and in their nation.

This, unfortunately, is happening right now! Because of the practices of some in the ministry (well-known and otherwise), many in the church no longer want to give tithes and offerings because of the abuses of those in church leadership. This has been so perverted by some that Christian men and women have refused to give of their finances because they have witnessed the perversion of these "corrupt" sons in the body of Christ that have disillusioned God's people.

I could not tell you how many times people have said things such as, "All preachers want is your money." They even go so far as to complain about one of the many televangelists that beg for money or one of the well-known preachers that have fallen. It is sad, but we (the modern church) have given the world and the "nay-sayers" plenty of ammunition in this area. We have also given the people of the church plenty of reasons to, "abhor the offering of the Lord," because of the way many of today's church leaders have lied and manipulated the people for more money.

These same "manipulators" often spend the money that is given to them in a manner that is unrighteous and wasteful as they live lavishly off the giving of the people. The Hophni and Phineas spirit is alive and thriving in many churches today, it is the leadership of the church that are to blame. It is sad to think that many carry the same attitudes and spirit of Hophni and Phinehas, bringing corruption into the church, and causing God's people to despise the offerings of the Lord.

The Wickedness of Eli's Sons

1 Samuel 2:22-25

[22] *Now Eli was very old, and he heard everything his sons did to all Israel, and how they lay with the women who assembled at the door of the tabernacle of meeting.*

[23] *So he said to them, "Why do you do such things? For I hear of your evil dealings from all the people.*

[24] *No, my sons! For it is not a good report that I hear. You make the LORD's people transgress.*

[25] *If one man sins against another, God will judge him. But if a man sins against the LORD, who will intercede for him?" Nevertheless, they did not heed the voice of their father because the LORD desired to kill them.*

Eli heard about everything his sons were doing, including how they were having sex with the women that came to the tabernacle to worship and/or work. He did nothing but give them a half-hearted scolding. Eli reprimanded his sons (they

6

were grown men at this point), but he did not do anything to remove them from being priests. Eli could have and should have removed his sons, at least until they repented and changed their behavior, but he did nothing except lecture his sons. As High Priest, Eli had the authority to do far more than merely scold his sons. He had the power to remove them and demand that they repent and be retrained as priests. Eli shows us what happens when a man is a weak father. He becomes a weak church leader as well. Eli did not show himself strong as a father, a spiritual leader, or a political leader. He had authority in all three of these arenas to remove his problem children from their ministry positions yet did little to correct the problem.

Many pastors and church leaders have very unruly children. This has become so prevalent that it is almost expected in many circles. The idea of the "PK" (preacher's kid) has become the running joke in the church world today. We expect the Preachers Kids to be the worst kids in the church, but also the most protected kids from the scrutiny of the church members. These PK's are allowed to act almost any way they want, and no one is supposed to say anything about it because that would embarrass the pastor. Yet the Bible has something very different to say about the church leader and his children.

1 Timothy 3:5

...for if a man does not know how to rule his own house, how will he take care of the church of God?

I have always wondered about this passage and why it seems so few live by it. We read about Eli and think, "He should have been removed from his office until he repented as a father and high priest." This should never be a mere thought, but it should

7

have been done. The people should have demanded this of him, but instead, he was allowed to remain in his position as these "corrupt sons" of his ruined the faith of the people entrusted to them.

How often do we see the "PK" (Preacher's Kid) act up in church? We can recognize the PK's by their terrible and unruly behavior and how the leadership shields them from correction. I know of churches where people were asked to step down from their positions in the church if they brought a complaint against any of the pastor's kids. I have been in churches where the pastor's kids were on drugs and/or, alcohol, were sleeping around with others in the church, etc. and the pastor was allowed to continue pastoring the church. 1 Timothy 3:5 should send chills down our spine and breed a healthy fear of the Lord in this area. It is time we take this verse and the passages like it very seriously. *Do not even get me started on the divorce rate among church leaders!*

Eli Has a Visitor

1 Samuel 2:29-34

> [29] *Why do you kick at My sacrifice and My offering which I have commanded in My dwelling place, and honor your sons more than Me, to make yourselves fat with the best of all the offerings of Israel My people?'*

> [30] *Therefore the LORD God of Israel says: 'I said indeed that your house and the house of your father would walk before Me forever.' But now the LORD says: 'Far be it from Me; for those who honor Me I will honor, and those who despise Me shall be lightly esteemed.*

^{31} *Behold, the days are coming that I will cut off your arm and the arm of your father's house so that there will not be an old man in your house.*

^{32} *And you will see an enemy in My dwelling place, despite all the good which God does for Israel. And there shall not be an old man in your house forever.*

^{33} *But any of your men whom I do not cut off from My altar shall consume your eyes and grieve your heart. And all the descendants of your house shall die in the flower of their age.*

^{34} *Now this shall be a sign to you that will come upon your two sons, on Hophni and Phinehas: in one day they shall die, both of them.*

Eli knew what his sons were doing, but he did nothing to stop them. On account of Hophni and Phinehas's continual rebellion and sin, and Eli's apathy and indifference towards his sons and their sin, God was going to purge the priesthood. God decided to kill Hophni and Phinehas in a single day (v.25). Eli's apathy towards the sins of his sons brought a death sentence upon them. Not only was God going to kill the sons of Eli, but his entire house, including his lineage, was going to pay the price for his failure as a father, priest, and judge.

Think about this and let it sink in for a moment. God was so angry with Eli and his two sons that He, the God of love, decided He was going to kill them for what they were doing to His chosen people. Meditate on this, God NEVER changes (Malachi 3:6; Hebrews 13:8). God was love at the time of Eli, and He is love today. God wanted Eli, and his sons removed because of their sin. It is hard for me to understand this, but it is nonetheless true. God was so incensed with Hophni and Phinehas that "the God of love" wanted to kill them. It is the same today when we see church leaders leading people astray because of their sin and apathy towards their own children. This is something that we have to come to terms with. This is something that should bring sobriety and clear thinking to our hearts and minds.

Many in today's church have a problem with the above truth. I've heard pastors and preachers say, "God would never kill anyone, because He is a God of love." It is unfortunate that there are those leading the church that claim to know and love God, but cannot reconcile this in their hearts and minds. It is *unloving* for God to keep these ones around. Hophni and Phinehas were akin to cancer in a body, and if left alone they could have destroyed the whole nation. Just as it is very loving to remove cancer from the natural body, it is also an expression of love to eliminate these corrupt priests from their position and from the nation. This goes for us today. If you ever become a "cancer" in the body of Christ, do not be surprised if you see God's surgical scalpel coming towards you. Do not run - REPENT!

Tolerated Sin Hinders the Prophetic

1 Samuel 3:1

> *Now the boy Samuel ministered to the LORD before Eli. And the word of the LORD was rare in those days; there was no widespread revelation.*

It was because of the sin of Hophni and Phinehas, and the apathetic attitude Eli had towards his sons, the Word of the Lord was "rare," and no "widespread revelation" was present. In this verse, the word "rare" points to its value as well as scarcity, and the phrase "widespread revelation" can be understood as, "a prophetic word that brings a breakthrough." The word of the

Lord (prophecy) was highly valued because it had become so rare (infrequent). The level of the prophetic that the people were left with was not as impactful as it once had been. By looking at the original language and meaning, it shows us that the word of the Lord was so rare that the prophets treated it as precious and costly gemstones. They longed for the word of the Lord that would cause the people of God to increase and have breakthrough in their lives and in the nation. This type of "widespread revelation" was rare because of the sin in the priesthood that was allowed to remain and increase.

Eli represents stagnant and lethargic spiritual leadership.

Hophni and Phinehas represent blatant, rebellious and sinful leadership.

The leadership of Eli and Hophni and Phinehas are wrong and will keep God's people from moving forward as they should. It is unfortunate, but we see these types of leaders in the modern church. Many Elis exist in the church today, and they are giving way to a Hophni and Phinehas type of leadership that is arising as well.

Just as it was at the time of Eli and his sons, we see similar consequences in our generation. Today we can find many prophetic voices, or at least many that proclaim, "Thus sayeth the Lord,"' but little (very little) breakthrough revelation is given. As I write this, many are scratching their head and wondering why the church in America is shrinking. It should be no mystery. People are leaving the church today for the same reason they were walking away from God's ordained standard of worship in

11

the days of Eli. People are simply fed-up with the sin, compromise, and complacency in the pulpit. People are fed up with the prophets (so-called) giving prophecies of little value. We need a breakthrough in this generation, and we, unfortunately, cannot find it in the church.

Do not misunderstand me. We have some great churches in America and some powerful prophetic voices, but is seems as if for every church that is functioning as it should, 100 other churches could be labeled "Eli." At the same time, for every true prophet, 100 other so-called prophets are muddying the waters. It is a tragedy when God's people have to strain out the mud and dirt of flesh and carnality merely to test a word to see if it is truly a word from God. Some great churches and true prophets can be found in America, but they, unfortunately, are not always recognized as they should be because of the nonsense around them.

During the time of Eli and his sons other priests would have existed, but only these three were spoken of. This is in part because Eli was the High Priest and Hophni and Phinehas were his sons, but the focus is on these three because of their sin. It is the same today. It seems that the church leaders that are "caught with their pants down" are the ones that make national and sometimes international news. Those falling and failing in the church make the news in the world around us because we have done such a bad job dealing with the sin in our own ranks. Many are doing fantastic jobs all around us, and we miss them because everyone is focused on those who are perpetually failing as a "priest."

When church leaders remain in their position too long, they often get lazy, fat, blind and apathetic to what is going on around them, as Eli did. They simply get comfortable in their position and as long as they are content they do not want to step down. This is a huge problem today. We have church leaders that have done a terrible job raising their children (both natural and spiritual children). It seems as if they are personally too comfortable in their position so, "Why rock the boat?" They are happy doing what they have always done so why change things? It is bad enough when a church leader gets "stuck," but when our position of comfort opens the door for sin and corruption, things must change. Something must happen to awaken us to our blindness, or God will be forced to act.

We need to remember that when God steps into a situation to correct what we have done and created, it is not always pretty. God will fix our mistakes, but at our expense. Many have a problem understanding this with today's "weak and spineless" doctrines that have permeated the church, but it is nonetheless true. God is not weak in this; nor will He cower. If He has to step in and take care of business, someone is in trouble.

Ichabod–the Glory Has Departed

Israel goes to war with the Philistines, and Hophni and Phinehas take the Ark of the Covenant to the camp of the Israelites. This would not have been a problem if they were not in open rebellion to God and His Word. Their disobedience and rebellion opened doors that should never have been opened.

1 Samuel 4:15-22

> [15] Eli was ninety-eight years old, and his eyes were so dim that he could not see.

13

¹⁶ *Then the man said to Eli, "I am he who came from the battle. And I fled today from the battle line." And he said, "What happened, my son?"*

¹⁷ *So the messenger answered and said, "Israel has fled before the Philistines, and there has been a great slaughter among the people. Also, your two sons, Hophni and Phinehas, are dead; and the ark of God has been captured."*

¹⁸ *Then it happened, when he made mention of the ark of God, that Eli fell off the seat backward by the side of the gate; and his neck was broken, and he died, for the man was old and heavy. And he had judged Israel forty years.*

¹⁹ *Now his daughter-in-law, Phinehas' wife, was with child, due to be delivered; and when she heard the news that the ark of God was captured, and that her father-in-law and her husband were dead, she bowed herself and gave birth, for her labor pains came upon her.*

²⁰ *And about the time of her death the women who stood by her said to her, "Do not fear, for you have borne a son." But she did not answer, nor did she regard it.*

²¹ *Then she named the child Ichabod, saying, "The glory has departed from Israel!" because the ark of God had been captured and because of her father-in-law and her husband.*

²² *And she said, "The glory has departed from Israel, for the ark of God has been captured."*

Not only did Hophni and Phinehas lose their lives in the battle just as God said, but the Ark of God was taken by the Philistines. When Eli hears of his sons and the capturing of the Ark, he fell off his seat, broke his neck and died. As I pointed out a moment ago, many have a difficult time wrapping their mind around this truth. If God has to step in because no one else will, the outcome will look much like this story above. Not only did the High Priest and his two sons die on that day, but the army of Israel was defeated and the Ark of the Covenant, which represents the presence of God, was taken from Israel. In one day the entire nation was brought to its knees because the political, religious, and military structures were completely devastated. To make matters worse, the presence of God left Israel. You talk about a major blow! Israel was in shambles.

Phinehas's wife was giving birth as all this was taking place, and she died during childbirth. This baby lost his mother, father, uncle, and grandfather; not to mention the priests that were to train and lead him, and the Ark of the Lord that represented God's presence and glory, all on the day he was born. It is very unfortunate, but this is happening all around us today.

The glory of God is all but gone in most churches. Church leaders are falling all around us as we are scrambling to keep our heads above water spiritually as well as financially. Our credibility is being destroyed by the culture we have been commissioned to impact as light and salt. The prophetic proclamations that are supposed to bring a breakthrough are doing little but stroking egos and tickling ears. All this is taking place, and some in the church still do not get it. They are scratching their heads wondering why the people are leaving the church. I am not sure if this is arrogance or ignorance; an unwillingness to face the truth in ourselves, or simply being oblivious of what the Bible actually says. Either way, things MUST change if we want the glory to return and remain.

As I have pointed out this is not merely a story of what happened in Israel 3,100 years ago, but it is a story of what is going on today. However, God is working in His church, clearing out the Elis that refuse to get their house and ministries in order. Why? Because if the house is not cleared of the weak and failing priesthood then we will never get to the place we need to be. God is restoring and ready to release His breakthrough visions and prophecies, but the compromise and apathy among the leaders must come down first. A purging has to come to the church before it is pure enough to adequately and righteously steward what is coming. Either the Elis, Hophnis and Phinehases of our age repent and change the way they conduct themselves, or they will be replaced by God Himself. God loves His people too much to leave us in the state we are in. Our God will move and shake the church, and when He does watch out!

After looking at this story and how it relates to us today it makes our present time seem very bleak at best, but God has a plan. As we find in the pages of the Bible, God does not remove something without bringing something better. God does not close one door without opening another. Our God has a beautiful way of clearing out the old to make way for something fresh, something bigger, and better, and will do what the old could not do. Do not let this chapter discourage you. Instead, allow it to challenge you in the way you do life and church. Are you tolerating sin in your own life and ministry? If so, REPENT! You can choose to remove the Eli, Hophni and Phinehas from your heart and life, or God will. Just remember what happens when it is left up to God alone to remove these from our midst.

Chapter 2
Raising Up Samuels

As we have found, the nation of Israel was sliding into sin and depravity while under the leadership of Eli and his two sons. This was because Eli, the High Priest and Judge, had allowed corruption to come into the priesthood primarily through his sons. Eli's two sons, Hophni and Phinehas, had positions as priests under their father and caused the people to sin because of their own sin. Eli knew of his sons' behavior and the result of their conduct, and did nothing about it. As a result of this, God sought to kill Hophni and Phinehas so that the priesthood could be restored.

One day a woman by the name of Hannah visited the tabernacle for prayer. This seemingly unimportant visit by this barren woman was the catalyst to Eli's undoing, as well the restoration of Israel back to God. It was through this woman that the answer to Israel's problems would be birthed. Through her travail of heart and body the answer came.

1 Samuel 1:9-18

> *⁹ So Hannah arose after they had finished eating and drinking in Shiloh. Now Eli the priest was sitting on the seat by the doorpost of the tabernacle of the LORD.*

> *¹⁰ And she was in bitterness of soul, and prayed to the LORD and wept in anguish.*

11 Then she made a vow and said, "O LORD of hosts, if You will indeed look on the affliction of Your maidservant and remember me, and not forget Your maidservant, but will give Your maidservant a male child, then I will give him to the LORD all the days of his life, and no razor shall come upon his head."

12 And it happened, as she continued praying before the LORD, that Eli watched her mouth.

13 Now Hannah spoke in her heart; only her lips moved, but her voice was not heard. Therefore Eli thought she was drunk.

14 So Eli said to her, "How long will you be drunk? Put your wine away from you!"

15 But Hannah answered and said, "No, my lord, I am a woman of sorrowful spirit. I have drunk neither wine nor intoxicating drink, but have poured out my soul before the LORD.

16 Do not consider your maidservant a wicked woman, for out of the abundance of my complaint and grief I have spoken until now."

17 Then Eli answered and said, "Go in peace, and the God of Israel grant your petition which you have asked of Him."

18 And she said, "Let your maidservant find favor in your sight." So the woman went her way and ate, and her face was no longer sad.

I find it interesting that Hannah is at the tabernacle with Eli as she is pouring out her heart before the LORD in prayer. Just as the Bible shows, she "was in bitterness of soul, and prayed to the LORD and wept in anguish." Clearly, she was expressing herself in a manner that displayed the hurt and pain she felt in her heart. Eli watches her and completely misses what was actually happening. Here before him was a woman in intercessory travail and he mistook it for drunkenness. The conclusion he came to regarding Hannah and her heartfelt prayer is sad on several levels. To mislabel fervent prayer is bad enough in itself, but to brand it as drunkenness is entirely another level of ignorance. It is probable that Eli had not seen such prayer at the Tabernacle in such a long time that he could not recognize it when it was right in front of him. Let us face it: if he was a man given to this type of prayer, he most likely would not have been found in the position of compromise that he was in. Had he been a man of prayer, as the spiritual leader of the nation more people would have followed his example and given themselves to prayer as well. Again, if fervent prayer such as Hannah's was not so rare, the priesthood would never have found itself in the situation it was in. If the priesthood were given to prayer, the nation would have given itself to prayer as well.

Recent studies have shown that the average prayer life of a church leader is about 30 minutes a day--30 minutes! Think about this for a moment and let it sink in. On average, most of the people that we call pastor only pray 30 minutes a day[1]. This also means that we will find church leaders that pray more than 30 minutes, but still others that pray less than 30 minutes. Pastors and church leaders may not like my next statement, but...that means that statistically the person you call 'Pastor' barely prays for you on a given day. If he or she is only praying 30 minutes a day you could have no one praying for you in any given day.

This should wake us all up and cause us all to change what we are doing as believers. Except for those that discipline

---

[1] http://churchleaders.com/pastors/pastor-articles/150915-u-s-statistics-on-prayer.html

themselves to pray, pastors and church leaders should be embarrassed about this. The pastors and church leaders that have failed in this area need to stand before their congregations and repent for this sin. These pastors and church leaders need to change the way they are leading the people, recognizing that they have failed in the essential elements of church leadership. We need to follow the example of Hannah.

Hannah was finally able to conceive and give birth to a male child. She named her son Samuel, which means, "heard of God." God heard her prayers and gave Hannah a son, but here is the catch – Hannah promised to give Samuel to the Lord all the days of his life.

1 Samuel 1:11

> "...give Your maidservant a male child, then I will give him to the LORD all the days of his life, and no razor shall come upon his head."

Hannah kept her promise to the Lord and gave Samuel to the Lord through Eli to be raised up in the tabernacle as a priest. As difficult as this was for her, Hannah fulfilled her promise by bringing Samuel to the tabernacle. Eli would from that point raise, teach, train, and nurture his replacement, because it was through Samuel that God was going to restore to Israel the "word of the Lord" as well as "widespread revelation."

Samuel was not an answer to the prayers of Hannah only. Many in Israel had been crying out because of the wicked priests. God Himself also was angry at what was happening with His people while under the leadership of Eli and his sons. God raised up Samuel to be the answer to Israel's problems.

This is often how God works. When a problem of this magnitude is found, God will raise up a prophet (or prophets) that will restore the people back to Him. Through Samuel, the political, religious, and financial institutions of Israel were to be restored to correct function. Through Samuel, God was restoring the breakthrough revelation that the nation needed in order flourish as it should.

1 Samuel 3:1-3

> [1] *Now the boy Samuel ministered to the LORD before Eli. And the word of the LORD was rare in those days; there was no widespread revelation.*
>
> [2] *And it came to pass at that time, while Eli was lying down in his place, and when his eyes had begun to grow so dim that he could not see,*
>
> [3] *and before the lamp of God went out in the tabernacle of the LORD where the ark of God was, and while Samuel was lying down,*

I do not want to focus only on the negative, but we need to establish and understand what the problems were at that time because we are facing much of the same challenges today. Eli and his sons represent much of today's church leadership. I have learned that you cannot fix what you are unwilling to face.

You cannot change
what you are reluctant to engage.

An example of this is, fewer and fewer Christians are exercising their right to vote in our elections. Because of those who refuse to vote our government is moving further away from God and His precepts. As the government rejects God, the nation as a whole is rejecting God as well. Now every aspect of our Christian heritage is under assault simply because so many of us do not want to face and fix the problems in the church. We have been ignoring the problems simply because the modern-day Elis are fat and comfortable in their positions.

> *What makes it worse is that many of our church leaders do not even recognize what the problem truly is, and because of that they have become part of the problem, not the solution.*

In 1 Samuel 3:2 it says this about Eli,

> *And it came to pass at that time, while Eli was lying down in his place, and when his eyes had begun to grow so dim that he could not see.*

This verse shows the spiritual condition of Eli, and in relationship to this, it shows the spiritual state of much of the modern church leadership in America. It is a sad, but true comparison.

Living in the Wrong Place

The statement, "in his place" represents the place that he made for himself, not the place that God wanted him to be. He had fashioned for himself a place of comfort and complacency, as he became fat, lethargic, and out of touch with the things that were going on around him. It is as if he developed a 'do not rock the boat' mentality because it was his boat that would have been rocked.

While Eli was "in his place", Samuel was in the presence of the Lord and did not even realize it. He was in the place where God was and had been receiving from His presence without understanding the implications of what that would mean. Samuel is far closer to the presence of the Lord while sleeping than Eli was when he was awake. The Ark represents the presence of God, and it was in God's presence that we find Samuel. Eli was in his place while Samuel was in HIS place.

1 Samuel 3:3 (NLT)

> *The lamp of God had not yet gone out, and Samuel was sleeping in the Tabernacle near the Ark of God.*

This shows us that Samuel, even before he knew the Lord, had been positioned to not only hear the voice of God but to restore the Word of the Lord and widespread revelation back to Israel. Just as Samuel was positioned to hear God and have an intimate relationship with Him, we too can place ourselves in a similar fashion. Instead of being in the place we create and make for ourselves, a place of comfort and conformity, we can be in the place where God's presence is manifest. In this "secret place," we will be able to hear from the Lord and bring the needed revelation to His people.

Eyes So Dim You Cannot See

Eli's eyes "had begun to grow so dim that he could not see." Eli had the inability to perceive and understand the time and season of his life and the time and season concerning the people of God. His blindness was more than a physical blindness; it was a spiritual blindness as well. Eli's blindness should have put him out of the priesthood, but he remained. The High Priest should have had clarity of vision physically, emotionally, and especially spiritually. Eli's eyes had gone dim in all three of these areas. Physically he was blind; emotionally he did not have the heart or courage to confront his sons regarding their sin; and spiritually he was blinded to the fact that God was about to deal with him and his sons in a severe manner. It is unfortunate, but so many in the church today have become blind spiritually, similar to Eli's blindness.

"Before the Lamp of God Went Out in the Tabernacle…"

This is the saving grace of this story. The "lamp" represents the revelation and illumination (widespread revelation) spoken of in verse three. Although no one was available to give this widespread revelation as God desired, and the lamp of revelation had grown dim, yet it was still burning.

The Law of God commanded that the Menorah (Lamp of God) was to "burn continuously" (Leviticus 24:1-3). The fact that the Bible says, "before the lamp of God went out in the tabernacle" shows that Eli did not keep the Menorah burning continuously as he was supposed to. Eli forsook the object that represents God's continual light, illumination, and revelation for His people, causing God to withdraw these very things from the priesthood.

Once a heart for God is gone from the spiritual leaders, it is gone from their followers as well

This principle is valid today, as it was back then. When God commands the leaders of His people to do something, the people will ultimately suffer if those leaders are disobedient and "blind" towards the will of God and the people they are to lead. It is the responsibility of the leader to live up to that title and lead by example. Spiritual leaders are to lead God's people into His will by being obedient to His word, and by teaching the people to do the same.

When a church leader refuses
to keep the fires of revelation burning,
the people will sit in darkness.

When leaders fail to bring illumination
of God's word and His will, the people will
begin to abhor what is holy.

As a result of the sin of Eli and his sons, Israel was left with a spiritual void. This vacuum kept the people of Israel from receiving the word of the Lord that would give them the power needed to break through the obstacles before them. The answer to this problem was found in Samuel. Samuel was being raised up in the house of Eli without being tainted by the sins of Eli. Many Samuels are being raised up right under the nose of the Elis of our day. God is about to release the Samuels, and they will restore the missing revelation and illumination of the Spirit that will bring much needed breakthroughs.

God Speaks to Samuel

1 Samuel 3:4-9

> ⁴ *that the LORD called Samuel. And he answered, "Here I am!"*
>
> ⁵ *So he ran to Eli and said, "Here I am, for you called me." And he said, "I did not call; lie down again." And he went and lay down.*
>
> ⁶ *Then the LORD called yet again, "Samuel!" So Samuel arose and went to Eli, and said, "Here I am, for you called me." He answered, "I did not call, my son; lie down again."*
>
> ⁷ *(Now Samuel did not yet know the LORD, nor was the word of the LORD yet revealed to him.)*
>
> ⁸ *And the LORD called Samuel again the third time. So he arose and went to Eli, and said, "Here I am, for you did call me." Then Eli perceived that the LORD had called the boy.*
>
> ⁹ *Therefore Eli said to Samuel, "Go, lie down; and it shall be, if He calls you, that you must say, 'Speak, LORD, for Your servant hears.'" So Samuel went and lay down in his place.*

This is the first time that God speaks to Samuel. Although Samuel heard the voice of God clearly, he was not able to distinguish His voice from others (namely Eli). This was not as strange as it may seem. Eli was not in a good place, but he was still the spiritual leader over Israel, and the one who raised and trained Samuel, so Samuel would make the connection to Eli in his heart when God spoke. Often the voice of God initially sounds like the voice of our fathers in the faith.

It is sad to note that Eli knew the voice of God and even perceived it (v.8); sad because he had lost the ability, because of sin, to hear God directly. Now a little boy was hearing God better than he was. I praise God when the young ones around me hear God's voice, but I cringe when they hear His voice when I do not. This causes me to purposely come closer to God and to seek His presence. If my spiritual children are hearing God better than I am, while they are still children, then I am in a bad place with God and need to return to His heart.

Many of you reading this need to take this to heart. You have been wondering why your spiritual kids are hearing God on a higher level than you. You have tried to make excuses for it, but the reality is that you have allowed other things to come in and your hearing is not as sharp as it used to be. It is time to get back into the intimacy with Christ you used to hunger and thirst for. It is time to come in and be fed of His Spirit spending time in His presence just as you have most likely taught your young ones to do. As you do this, God will take you to higher heights, and you will take your spiritual children with you.

1 Samuel 3:10-11

> [10] Now the LORD came and stood and called as at other times, "Samuel! Samuel!" And Samuel answered, "Speak, for Your servant hears."

> [11] Then the LORD said to Samuel: "Behold, I will do something in Israel at which both ears of everyone who hears it will tingle.

Samuel now hears the word of the Lord, and thanks to Eli, Samuel perceives that it is actually God speaking. God promises Samuel that He is going to do something powerful in Israel, "at which the ears of everyone who hears it will tingle." Why the ears?

Because God is going to restore the prophetic word through Samuel (among other things).

1 Samuel 3:12-15

> ¹² *In that day I will perform against Eli all that I have spoken concerning his house, from beginning to end.*
>
> ¹³ *For I have told him that I will judge his house forever for the iniquity which he knows, because his sons made themselves vile, and he did not restrain them.*
>
> ¹⁴ *And therefore I have sworn to the house of Eli that the iniquity of Eli's house shall not be atoned for by sacrifice or offering forever."*
>
> ¹⁵ *So Samuel lay down until morning and opened the doors of the house of the LORD. And Samuel was afraid to tell Eli the vision.*

It must have been a difficult thing for Samuel to hear this about the man that was like a father to him physically as well as spiritually. As difficult as this was, Samuel got a crash course in the prophetic word of the Lord. The word of the Lord is not always easy and filled with blessings, but it always produces what God wants it to. This revelation of what God was about to do to the house of Eli may have been difficult for Samuel to handle. Hearing what God said caused him to grow and understand the need to be in right standing with God. It also revealed the demand of being the premier prophet of the land. This was a massive thing for him to carry and God gave it all to him in his inaugural revelation.

When Samuel received the revelation of what God was about to do to Eli and his sons, he also received a revelation about how he would come into the position he was being prepared for.

Samuel could not take his rightful place until Eli was removed. What I find surprising about Samuel is that he never rejoiced about Eli's demise. Samuel was "afraid to tell Eli the vision." I believe he was afraid because of his love for Eli. I am sure he knew that things had to change, and he knew that Eli was warned by God as well as other prophets (1 Samuel 2:27-36) about his sin and the sins of his sons, but Samuel received impartation from this man and loved him deeply.

I have had men in my life that became as spiritual fathers to me that got off course. It was disheartening to me when God showed me what was to take place in their life if they did not repent. I watched one fall deeper and deeper into sin and the depravity of sexual sin until it killed him. The whole time I was heartbroken because I watched as this one that meant so much to me, and that had imparted into my life and ministry, was destroyed right before my eyes. The truly tragic thing about it was he was warned by several people about the course he was taking, and yet he continued until it ruined him. Even as I write this, my heart breaks because of what he meant to me. I am also reminded of why we must stay close to God and follow His Word at all times and at all costs.

Samuel Grows & The Word of the Lord is Restored

1 Samuel 3:19-21

¹⁹ So Samuel grew, and the LORD was with him and let none of his words fall to the ground.

²⁰ And all Israel from Dan to Beersheba knew that Samuel had been established as a prophet of the LORD.

21 Then the LORD appeared again in Shiloh. For the LORD revealed Himself to Samuel in Shiloh by the word of the LORD.

Even before the death of Eli and his sons Samuel grew and matured in the things of the Lord. As it says, *"the LORD was with him and let none of his words fall to the ground."* This shows us that Samuel was pure in his prophetic gift and that God completely trusted him. All the people knew that he was truly a prophet. Also, *"the LORD appeared again in Shiloh. For the LORD revealed Himself to Samuel in Shiloh by the word of the LORD."*

Shiloh = *a place of rest*

The word Shiloh speaks prophetically of the place where God meets with His people, and vice versa. This is not merely being at rest yourself, but being at the place where God finds rest. When we can come and rest in His presence, we will be able to not only hear God better, but we will be entrusted with the things needed to restore the church and bring her to where she needs to be.

Through Samuel, God was restoring true worship. Not one-sided dead worship, but worship that included revelatory interaction with God. Not only was a new dynamic in spiritual things now in place, but it impacted every other aspect of community life. The revelations that brought breakthrough that the nation needed was now flowing freely through Samuel.

So powerful was Samuel that everything he said came to pass – EVERYTHING! Samuel carried within him the Word that pierced through all darkness and that could not be stopped. Once the Word of the Lord was released from his lips, it was so.

A great revolution is coming to the body of Christ. Little 'Samuels' are being raised up right under Eli's nose, but these Samuels will not be small for long. They have been growing in the power and grace of God with the piercing Word of the Lord within them, as it was in Samuel. They will have the authority of God in them to the point that their words will never fail. What they say will be forever established. Do not rejoice in this too much yet, because the first groups that will hear their word are the Elis among us. Judgment begins in the household of God, and these Samuels will be the ones that brings the word of judgment into the house.

1 Peter 4:17

> *For the time has come for judgment to begin at the house of God; and if it begins with us first, what will be the end of those who do not obey the gospel of God?*

Keep in mind that judgment begins at the top as well. Not only is it coming to the house of God first, but to those who are the leaders in the house. Remember, just as it was with Eli and his sons, it will be with the church leadership of today.

Chapter 3
Restoring the Word of the Lord

Samuel the Prophet was used of God to restore the Word of the Lord and the vision that brings breakthrough. Israel had been brought out of its spiritual stupor because of the ministry of Samuel. It is interesting to see what God uses to restore His people spiritually. Revival in Israel came through a prophet. Samuel the Prophet was the catalyst used to reestablish the prophetic word of the Lord that brought the needed breakthroughs in the nation. These advances helped to bring the people back to God and back to the way God wanted them to serve Him. This is a principle we all should be aware of.

Pray for the prophets to arise and the restoration of the prophecies that bring breakthrough in our nation.

After reading through the book of Acts it is obvious that the church today does not operate and function with the same power and authority of the first-century church. Just as in the time of Eli, much of the spiritual power that we once walked in and enjoyed is gone. Many have developed doctrines trying to explain away our powerlessness, but we have lost our power because of the Elis in the church.

Over the centuries we have lost such things as healing, miracles, tongues (all the gifts of the Spirit), along with the office gifts of apostle and prophet. Not in every corner of today's church, but in many sects of Christianity these things are completely gone, and many have even called these things demonic (of the devil). It is a sad day when the moving of the Holy Spirit is considered to be demonic by those who call themselves Christian. This is the same type of thing that was taking place under the leadership of Eli and his sons. Hophni and Phinehas were doing things that caused the people to abhor the offering of the Lord (1 Samuel 2:17).

> *The very things that God set in place to bring*
> *His people to Him, the people now despised*
> *because of the sin and failures of the priesthood.*

The principles remain the same today. Some Christians abhor the things of God because of failed and faulty teaching from the modern priesthood. When we hear from the pulpit such things as, "speaking in tongues is of the devil," it sets us up for failure and spiritual weakness. People begin to abhor and turn away from things that are freely given us by God. Every gift of the Spirit is given by God to build up and edify the church.

1 Corinthians 14:12

Even so, you, since you are zealous for spiritual gifts, let it be for the edification of the church that you seek to excel.

1 Corinthians 14:26

How is it then, brethren? Whenever you come together, each of you has a psalm, has a teaching, has a tongue, has a revelation, has an interpretation. Let all things be done for edification.

These gifts and the power that goes with them are given to cause growth in the body of Christ. Increase in numbers, but also in maturity. When we reject the gifts that were given for our benefit, we all suffer. Think of it this way: how many people have died prematurely because of the erroneous teaching that healing is not for today? How many people have suffered and struggled with addictions that could have been easily broken from their life, but were taught that miracles and deliverance are a thing of the past? Also, think of the powerful revelations that could have been received by those who believe tongues are of the devil, or that the move of the Holy Spirit is a thing of the past. If the 'priests' of today had their doctrine and theology correct, the church would be far more powerful today than it is presently. It is Hophni and Phinehas all over again.

When we remove the gifts and power of the Spirit from the church, we eliminate the tools and materials needed to edify and build up the church.

Without these the church is small and weak; not necessarily small in size, but small in influence and power.

Restoration of the Word of the Lord

1 Samuel 3:19-21

> [19] *So Samuel grew, and the LORD was with him and let none of his words fall to the ground.*

20 And all Israel from Dan to Beersheba knew that Samuel had been established as a prophet of the LORD.

21 Then the LORD appeared again in Shiloh. For the LORD revealed Himself to Samuel in Shiloh by the word of the LORD.

Even before the death of Eli and his sons, Samuel grew and matured in the things of the Lord. As it says, "the LORD was with him and let none of his words fall to the ground." This shows us that Samuel was pure in his prophetic gift and that God completely trusted him. Samuel was not one to 'play' with his gift. He walked as a prophet and kept himself in the purity of God and the fear of the Lord. Samuel did not use his gift for personal gain (as we often see today), but spoke only what God told him to speak. All the people knew that he truly was a prophet, because of the purity of his heart, life, and gift. God trusted Samuel because his heart was towards Him.

I remember a time while visiting a particular church, the 'prophet' (debatable) was getting ready to prophesy to the people in the church. He announced that three ministry lines would be formed. The first ministry line was the $20 a word line; the second line was the $50 line, and the third was the $100 line. If you only wanted a $20 word, then you would get in that line. However, if you wanted the mega-prophecy you better get in the $100 line. As disgusting as it is, this type of thing happens more often than we want to admit. It is sad to think that some in the church today do this sort of thing, but even more upsetting is that people still attend these churches. Personally, that would have been my last Sunday in that church if I was a member.

Today, God is raising up Samuels that will be pure in their gift and that will bring the church to the place she is supposed to be. The church today is to operate and function in great and

36

awesome power: the power of God to change lives and set the captives free. This will not happen until we fully embrace the Word of God and once again exercise that power in such a way that the world knows we serve a God in heaven, and show His love through these power encounters. None of this will be a reality until we operate in our gifts in the same holiness and purity that Samuel did. The fear of the Lord must once again permeate the body of Christ to the point that we repent of these silly, foolish, and sinful practices that besmirch the gifts and their proper use. We need the Samuels of our day to rise up in righteousness and power.

Remember, Shiloh = a place of rest

Often when speaking about the 'rest' of the Lord, people envision hammocks by the ocean while drinking an iced tea. As great as this sounds, it is not necessarily Shiloh, the rest of the Lord. The true Shiloh is a spiritual place, a Spirit-filled place.

> *Shiloh represents that place where we come into such intimate relationship with God that we are fed and strengthened by His Spirit and presence, and where He is fed by our presence.*

It is unfortunate, but many will never understand that last statement, "where He is fed by our presence." God so desires to meet with us that He creates and establishes a "secret place" where we can meet together. It is in the secret place of intimate worship and relationship that His presence feeds us and our presence will feed Him. Not with food per se', but with things that are spiritual and on a much deeper level. God finds pleasure in His people when we enter in and give Him what He desires. In that secret place, He will pour out His Spirit to those who have connected with Him on those deeper levels. This is the 'rest' of the Lord; this is Shiloh.

Israel Wants a King

1 Samuel 8:1-9

> ¹ *Now it came to pass when Samuel was old that he made his sons judges over Israel.*

> ² *The name of his firstborn was Joel, and the name of his second, Abijah; they were judges in Beersheba.*

> ³ *But his sons did not walk in his ways; they turned aside after dishonest gain, took bribes, and perverted justice.*

> ⁴ *Then all the elders of Israel gathered together and came to Samuel at Ramah,*

> ⁵ *and said to him, "Look, you are old, and your sons do not walk in your ways. Now make us a king to judge us like all the nations."*

> ⁶ *But the thing displeased Samuel when they said, "Give us a king to judge us." So Samuel prayed to the LORD.*

> ⁷ *And the LORD said to Samuel, "Heed the voice of the people in all that they say to you; for they have not rejected you, but they have rejected Me, that I should not reign over them.*

> ⁸ *According to all the works which they have done since the day that I brought them up out of Egypt, even to this day — with which they have forsaken Me and served other gods — so they are doing to you also.*

> ⁹ *Now, therefore, heed their voice. However, you shall solemnly forewarn them, and show them the behavior of the king who will reign over them."*

We found that the transition from Eli to Samuel was set off primarily by Eli's failures as a father. The things that caused him to fail as a father also caused him fail as High Priest. Samuel was a prophet that was righteous in his prophetic office, but he was weak as a parent. Samuel's sons turned out like Eli's sons, "his sons did not walk in his ways; they turned aside after dishonest gain, took bribes, and perverted justice." The fear of the Lord was present with Samuel regarding his prophetic gift and office, but not as a father. What Samuel exercised in the spirit he could not seem to master in the natural, regarding his children.

This is a huge problem in the church today. Many church leaders are raising children that would fit the description of Hophni, Phinehas, Joel, and Abijah. Many are failing regarding their parenting even though their ministries seem healthy and intact. It is a sad truth, but many children feel abandoned by their parents that are in the ministry, and this is particularly the case with the men in ministry. Many wives have been abandoned by husbands that are quick to run off to people in need, never seeming to care that they are leaving their family in need.

A pastor once stepped into the pulpit of his church and proceeded to tell his congregation that he is resigning from his position as pastor at the church. He told the congregation that he was resigning because he had an affair. After the gasps, the angry and nervous stares, and the murmuring begins he proceeds to tell the church that he did not have an affair with another woman but with them—the church. Now, of course, everyone was scratching their head and wondering what he meant as if it was a joke, but sadly it was no joke at all.

The pastor went on to share how he had spent so much time at the church and with the people of the church that he had neglected his wife and children. He explained that his wife had spent many lonely nights waiting for him to come home from his many counseling appointments and hospital visits. The pastor told them that his kids had to go with mom alone to their ball games because most of his Saturdays were spent at the church mowing lawns, fixing the plumbing, and doing the administrative work of the church. When he was finished speaking everyone knew that he was correct. This pastor truly had an affair, and they all needed to repent for it. This pastor walked away from that church so he could get his home and family together.

1 Timothy 3:2-5

> *2 A bishop then must be blameless, the husband of one wife, temperate, sober-minded, of good behavior, hospitable, able to teach;*
>
> *3 not given to wine, not violent, not greedy for money, but gentle, not quarrelsome, not covetous;*
>
> *4 one who rules his own house well, having his children in submission with all reverence*
>
> *5 (for if a man does not know how to rule his house, how will he take care of the church of God?);*

It is my prayer that we as the people of God will grow and mature in all aspects. For those of us that are not doing right by our family, we must change the way we do things and stop neglecting our spouses and children, or simply get out of the ministry position we presently hold. This will give us the time we need to actually lead our families, and it will allow someone else to take our place in the church; someone whose priorities are in order. It is time for those in church leadership to take I Timothy

3:5 very seriously. If we cannot rule our own home, then how can we take care of God's home? We cannot rule our home correctly if we are absent.

Samuel was a fantastic prophet, but a terrible father. Why was he such a bad parent? He obtained his parental skills from watching Eli. This shows that we must break the negative things in our generation so that it is not passed on to the next generation. If we do not take care of our weaknesses and failures today, our children may make the same mistakes. Not only that, but it can be passed to our grandchildren and great-grandchildren as well. Someone must break the negative patterns before it is passed on to future generations. The next generation should inherit blessings from the previous generation, never curses. Had Samuel recognized what caused Eli's sons to become wicked, he may have raised his sons differently.

Eli's weakness as a father led the people of Israel to, "abhor the offering of the Lord." Samuel's weakness as a father caused the people of Israel to want a "king to judge us like all the nations." The people of Israel wanted a change in the governmental structure of the nation because Samuel followed in the footsteps of Eli in his parenting. No longer did the people want God as their king, but they wanted to lower themselves to the level of the nations around them. This decision is traced directly back to Samuel's parenting skills. Joel and Abijah could have been removed as judges at any time by Samuel, but he neglected his duties as the premier judge and as a father. Now the people want to remove God's governmental system and replace it with a worldly system, all because of the weak parenting skills of one man.

No matter how healthy a church or ministry may seem, look no further than the spouse and children of the head of that organization. The strength of a church leader is seen in his/her spouse and children. I have had to walk away from people because of how they treated those closest to them. I have learned to first look at the overall health of a man's family and household before getting too involved with him. His organization may seem like it is doing everything right, but if it is at the cost of his family, it is not worth the price. Unfortunately, not enough people in the church today are strong enough to walk away from leaders that are not setting the example regarding their home and family. Let's face it. If believers were to leave a church based solely on how the children of the church leadership behave, many churches would be empty. Someone has to have a backbone and start walking away from these failing fathers. These church leaders would be forced to take a look at their parenting skills before their ministries completely fail. In light of this, it is not unloving to say, "Pastor, I can no longer be part of your church as long as your children are so unruly and your wife is so unhappy. Get your house in order, and I'll be back." This could actually be the most loving thing a church leader hears.

It is NEVER right to leave THE church (the Body of Christ), but sometimes it is right to leave a church (a local Assembly)

If sin is in the pastor's life that he refuses to repent of and change, then leave that church and find one that is led by someone that is humble enough to follow God as he should. This should NEVER give anyone license to "church hop" or to become judgmental and manipulative of church leadership. It should, however, open our eyes to the reality that we all are responsible for the overall health of our churches.

When the people no longer wanted the judges over them, but instead wanted a king, Samuel felt rejected and betrayed. This is understandable since the people, in essence, told Samuel, "We no longer want you or those like you to rule over us. Oh, and we want you to find your replacement for us." I know that I would be a little emotional if I were in Samuel's shoes. As crushing as this may have been this is what God said to Samuel, *"Heed the voice of the people in all that they say to you; for they have not rejected you, but they have rejected Me, that I should not reign over them."* By rejecting Samuel, the people have actually rejected God and His will for them. Samuel was the judge that spoke on behalf of God, their King.

Reject the one that the King sends,
and you have actually rejected the King Himself.

It is wise to understand this principle:
if we reject God's way of doing things,
we reject God.

God is always part of the system He designs.

When He gives a command,
we need to understand that He is found
within the command.

For this reason obedience to His word is so paramount. We discover God and are brought into a deeper relationship with Him when we are obedient to His Word. This goes for what we see written in the Bible as well as what He speaks to us in person. His presence is found by those who are obedient to Him.

> ### *The greater the obedience,*
> ### *the greater His presence.*

God could see the bigger picture. He knew that it was only a matter of time before the Israelites wanted a king. As a matter of fact, He was fully prepared for this moment, even having Moses write and speak about it and include it in the Law.

Deuteronomy 17:14-15

> [14] *"When you come to the land which the LORD your God is giving you, and possess it and dwell in it, and say, 'I will set a king over me like all the nations that are around me,' [15] you shall surely set a king over you whom the LORD your God chooses; one from among your brethren you shall set as king over you; you may not set a foreigner over you, who is not your brother.*

God put this in His Word about 200 years before the people asked for a king. God knew this was going to happen. This was just another way that the people set up an idol and served another god. While journeying through the desert, the people made a golden calf and worshiped it as god (Exodus 32:1-35). No image or physical idol was present, but they and their will became their god. They rejected the Word of the Lord for their own word. When people choose their own will over the will of God, they make themselves into the object of their worship. They become a god unto themselves.

1 Samuel 8:8

> *According to all the works which they have done since the day that I brought them up out of Egypt, even to this day — with*

which they have forsaken Me and served other gods – so they are doing to you also.

God points out the people have a pattern of forsaking Him and serving other gods. God goes on to say, "so they are doing to you also." The people wanted a king just like the nations around them, instead of a Judge that judges with the heart of God, and whose word never fails. It is interesting that the people never came to Samuel with a heart to fix the real problem. The problem was not Samuel, but it was his sons. Samuel's sons, *"did not walk in his ways; they turned aside after dishonest gain, took bribes, and perverted justice."* The elders of Israel should have wanted to stay faithful to God's design of having judges over them, but also should have wanted new judges that would judge the people righteously. This would have been the correct course of action to take. The elders could have said, "Samuel we love you and know you judge the nation in righteousness. We will not have your sons as judges over us. Find us new judges that will make righteous judgments, and that will live righteously themselves." It is never OK to reject God's way of doing things simply because things are not going as they should. We are to establish our churches, ministries, and homes as God would have them established. When things begin to go off course, we are to get it back on course and to God's original design.

We are never allowed to trash the whole thing, but to rectify the problem areas and repair what is broken and no longer working.

We are to bring everything back into God's order and design.

It is unfortunate to see the course of many churches in America. Some churches no longer care if the church leadership has a theology degree because they are looking for leadership with marketing degrees. Churches and church boards will use marketability as criteria for finding a pastor to lead the church, instead of the knowledge of the Bible. It is sad to think that a person could be rejected as a church leader, not because they lack a solid understanding of the Bible, but because they do not have a marketing degree, or because they simply do not have that TV look about them. Churches like this can become mega-churches in a very short period of time, only to find that they have a church full of people that do not even understand the basic tenets of Christianity. This is a sad but true reality today. I have visited some large churches that seem to have it all together, but unfortunately God cannot be found. They have exchanged the presence of God for the look and hype that captures the attention of the flesh of man. It is a good principle to remember,

Whatever brought the people in
will be what keeps them.

Bring them in by the flesh, and it will be the flesh that holds them. Bring the people in by the Spirit, and it will be the Spirit that sustains them.

We have failed as church leaders when the people desire a church that is watered down and not deeply spiritual. When the people in our churches no longer want a move of the Spirit, but are happy with another program, we have done something very wrong as leaders. Our ministry and leadership styles should leave the people hungry for the deeper things of God. If our people are satisfied with shallow ear-tickling messages, look no further than the pulpit.

2 Timothy 4:1-4

¹ I charge you therefore before God and the Lord Jesus Christ, who will judge the living and the dead at His appearing and His kingdom:

² Preach the word! Be ready in season and out of season. Convince, rebuke, exhort, with all longsuffering and teaching.

³ For the time will come when they will not endure sound doctrine, but according to their own desires, because they have itching ears, they will heap up for themselves teachers;

⁴ and they will turn their ears away from the truth, and be turned aside to fables.

When the people want a soft word over a life-changing word, we have failed. At this point, the leadership MUST repent and turn away from the shallow watered-down teaching, or be replaced as we see here with Samuel. It is never enough to merely be able to move in the power gifts as Samuel did. The power gifts MUST come through a vessel that is honoring to God, or it will eventually corrupt the people.

When the people are no longer being fed as they should be it will not be long before they start asking for things that may never give them what they truly need. This is the case with Israel and the sons of Samuel. First, the priesthood was corrupt, and it caused the people to abhor the offering. Then they experienced corruption in the judicial and political system causing the people to want something other than God to rule over them. In both cases, it was the fault of the religious leaders that set off these events.

God Gives the People a King

When the leadership no longer functions as God intends it to, the people will want something else to replace it. God was the King of Israel, but His representatives continued to misrepresent Him, causing the people to want something else. Now, because of Samuel's sons and their corruption the people wanted a king like all the other nations. Is it not interesting that failed leadership causes the people to want to look like everyone else? Instead of wanting to be better and to rise above the other nations, failed leadership causes the people to want to be average and ordinary, like everyone else. On account of Samuel's failures as a father and judge, the people want a king just like everyone else. So what does God do? He gives them what they ask for. By the way...

> ### *Be careful of what you ask for,*
> ### *you might just get it.*

1 Samuel 9:1-2

> *[1] There was a man of Benjamin whose name was Kish, the son of Abiel, the son of Zeror, the son of Bechorath, the son of Aphiah, a Benjamite, a mighty man of power.*
>
> *[2] And he had a choice and handsome son whose name was Saul. There was not a more handsome person than he among the children of Israel. From his shoulders upward he was taller than any of the people.*

God chose Saul to be the new king over Israel. God gave the people of Israel everything they wanted in a king.

For example:

48

- Saul came from a wealthy and prosperous family.
- Saul's father Kish was known as a "mighty man of power."
- Saul was a "choice and handsome" man.
- Saul was "taller than any of the people."

Saul was everything that the people would want in a king, and that was the problem.

> *Saul was everything "the people" wanted*
> *in a king.*

The people of Israel lowered themselves to the surrounding nations. God had established them as "the head and not the tail"; they were to be, "above only, and not be beneath (Deuteronomy 28:13; 44)", but they could not see themselves in that manner. The sin of the sons of Samuel caused the people to want to be just like everyone else.

It is a sad day when the people of God want to be just like the world around them because we have been created for greatness. When we accept Christ, the power of His salvation and Spirit compels us to be and to do the extraordinary.

> *When the people who are marked for greatness*
> *settle for the typical and ordinary, everyone*
> *loses, especially the world around us.*

Those around us will no longer have anything righteous to aspire to. We will claim to represent Christ while making Him look the same as every other religious figure.

As the Body of Christ makes its transition from the minor things to the greater things, we must keep in mind that other indicators beyond the anointing point to good or bad leadership. It has been a problem in the church for many years; we tend to look at the anointing of a person as the marker for quality ministry. Anointing is important, but an even more important indicator of healthy ministry exists, and it is called character!

Matthew 7:16

> *You will know them by their fruits. Do men gather grapes from thornbushes or figs from thistles?*

Matthew 7:20

> *Therefore by their fruits, you will know them.*

Notice that Jesus says that we will know them by the fruit of their lives — their character — NOT the anointing they operate in. Character is of the greatest importance when it comes to leadership.

> *The anointing empowers a person for a leadership role, but it is the quality of character that makes a leader trustworthy to those that follow them.*

Leaders do not fail because of a lack of anointing. Where one lacks power, they simply can surround themselves with people of power.

Leaders fail because of a lack of character.

Character can be described as, "qualities of honesty, courage, integrity or the like." These are the types of fruit we should be cultivating in our own life, as well as the fruit we should be looking for in the lives of our leadership. Of course, we want charismatic and powerful leaders, but these qualities fall short in comparison to someone with exemplary character.

The sons of Samuel, Joel, and Abijah were sorely lacking in their character. They most likely had all the other qualities of a great leader, but lacking character is what pushed the people over the edge, causing them to reject God's governmental system. This is the danger of leadership without integrity.

The people we are to lead will eventually walk away from God and His will if we allow these types of leaders to remain in their position. It is time for the real leaders in the church to rise up and deal with the lack of integrity in those who are lacking in their character. We can no longer stand by and watch as God's people turn from God's truth because they can no longer find it in the leadership over them. It is time for us to remove the Hophnis, Phinehases, Joels, and Abijahs from the church before the people completely reject God's system for one that mirrors the world. Some might say that it is already too late.

Chapter 4
The Donkey Hunter

As we have been looking at the spiritual and political changes in Israel (beginning with Eli), we realize that the political changes and the spiritual changes were very much connected. What was happening spiritually soon affected the politics of the nation as well. This is something that we must realize in our modern age. What is going on spiritually will eventually manifest in every other area of culture and society. Often people get it backward. It is not politics that affect the spiritual nature of our society, as much as the spiritual nature affects the political realm of the society. Where you have corruption in the church, you will soon see corruption in government as well as in business and the home.

A weak church always leads
to a corrupt society.

Eli allowed corruption to come into the priesthood because of his careless attitude regarding his sons and their sin. This gave rise to Samuel. Samuel was a great prophet and judge, but he failed with his sons in a similar fashion as Eli. As great as Samuel was as a prophet, he did what Eli had done with the position of authority entrusted to him. Samuel allowed corruption to enter into the system of the judges (political). Samuel himself was not corrupt, but his two sons were. As judges, the sons of Samuel perverted justice for their own gain. This led to the people wanting to replace God as King with a king "like all the other nations." God gave His people what they wanted, and chose Saul to be the first King of Israel. This is a clear picture of what happens in a society when the church refuses to deal with sin and corruption in its ranks. The people of the church, as well as the society, in general, will reject even the good that is in the church if the sin is not dealt with. Else they will become lethargic toward the sin in their leaders, giving them an excuse to remain in sin themselves. This, unfortunately, is all too common in our day and age.

Saul...The Donkey Hunter

1 Samuel 9:3-5

> ³ Now the donkeys of Kish, Saul's father, were lost. And Kish said to his son Saul, "Please take one of the servants with you, and arise, go and look for the donkeys."
>
> ⁴ So he passed through the mountains of Ephraim and through the land of Shalisha, but they did not find them. Then they passed through the land of Shaalim, and they were not there. Then he passed through the land of the Benjamites, but they did not find them.
>
> ⁵ When they had come to the land of Zuph, Saul said to his servant who was with him, "Come, let us return, lest my father cease caring about the donkeys and become worried about us."

It is interesting to note that on the way to being the first King of Israel, Saul was chasing donkeys. This may not seem imperative to the overall story about the future King of Israel, but God thought it important enough to include it in His eternal word. This portion is important in that it sets the stage for the rest of the story. It helps us to understand what type of man Saul was. Saul was not a bad person. He was chosen by God to be the king that would replace God as king to Israel. We do not always look at it in this light, but that is what happened. The people wanted to replace God, the Heavenly King, with a man, an earthly king. Simply put, the people rejected God as their King.

1 Samuel 8:7

> And the LORD said to Samuel, "Heed the voice of the people in all that they say to you; for they have not rejected you, but they have rejected Me, that I should not reign over them.

We hear stories all the time of people being replaced on the job, and as they are about to leave they are expected to train their replacements. This is, in essence, what was taking place. The people no longer wanted God and His representatives to reign over them, so they asked for a king to rule over them like the nations around them. It was God that found Saul to be king over the people. It was God who had to locate the one that would replace Himself as king. He found Saul who was the best person in all of Israel for that position at that time. God did not look for someone that did not have the potential to be a great king; instead, He found the best that Israel had to offer at that time, to serve Him and the people as the King of Israel. Saul had the makings of a great king that could serve God, the people, and their purposes very well. God was not vengeful in His thinking when He found Saul. As a matter of fact, it was the exact opposite. God found the best person for the job, knowing that even the best they had to offer still paled in comparison to the leadership He provided through the system He developed.

We are introduced to Saul as he was out looking for his father's donkeys that had wandered off. After three days of searching (1 Samuel 9:20), Saul is ready to return home, concerned that his father would become worried about him. Keep in mind that this is going to be the first King of Israel. The soon to be King of Israel was looking for his father's donkeys that had wandered off. We have no record of how these donkeys had escaped, but one thing we know for sure, someone was not doing their job. Someone failed to watch over the donkeys as they should have. This story shows, that no matter why these animals escaped, Saul and his servant were looking for them for three days. After three days of searching Saul and his servant were still empty handed.

Why did it take so long for someone to realize that the donkeys were missing? Why did Kish, Saul's father, have to tell Saul to go looking for them? Why did not Saul know about these missing donkeys before this and bring them back sooner?

We may never know the answer to these questions this side of heaven, but these issues are valid when looking at the future king. These donkeys were Saul's responsibility simply because Saul was to inherit everything from his father. These were Saul's donkeys as well, not merely his father's donkeys. This portion of the story gives us a glimpse into the quality and character of Saul. Does that part of the story reveal the makings of a great king? Even still, he was the best Israel had to offer.

From Donkey Hunter to a Prophet

After searching for the donkeys for three days, Saul is ready to go home. Saul says to the servant, *"Come, let us return, lest my father cease caring about the donkeys and become worried about us (1 Samuel 9:3)"*. Saul became more concerned about the feelings of his father than his financial well-being. These donkeys were not pets but represented the business that Kish was involved in, and these donkeys were part of the family business. Saul knew his father would become worried and this bothered Saul to the point of wanting to give up on their quest to find the donkeys and to restore the family business. Saul's heart and mind were fixed on the immediate moment, not the future. Saul was focused on how his absence was making his father feel at the moment, not what the loss of the donkeys might mean to the family financially.

This is another problem that arose then and has plagued the modern church. Far too many church leaders are more concerned with the feelings of their congregation than their overall well-being. The politically correct mindset that has permeated our culture and society is alive and well in the church today. Many church leaders refuse to speak about turning from sin (and naming it), living righteously, walking in purity, etc., because it may offend someone.

Recently I read an article that a president of a Christian college wrote to the entire student body of his school. It came after a student approached him because this student was offended at the speaker in the chapel when he spoke about sin and the consequences of sin. The student wanted the president to stop bringing these types of speakers into the school. You know the kind of speakers that tell the truth. I was happy to read that the president of the school dealt with this mentality in a straightforward, firm manner.

We as the church, especially church leaders, must stop worrying about the immediate feelings of the people around us and start telling the whole truth regardless of who gets offended. Our 'offensive truth' may actually keep people from going to hell and being eternally separated from God. Like Saul, many refuse to look at the big picture regarding others' overall well-being.

A Wise Servant

1 Samuel 9:6-10

> [6] And he said to him, "Look now, there is in this city a man of God, and he is an honorable man; all that he says surely comes to pass. So let us go there; perhaps he can show us the way that we should go."

> [7] Then Saul said to his servant, "But look if we go, what shall we bring the man? For the bread in our vessels is all gone, and there is no present to bring to the man of God. What do we have?"

> [8] And the servant answered Saul again and said, "Look, I have here at hand one-fourth of a shekel of silver. I will give that to the man of God, to tell us our way."

> [9] (Formerly in Israel, when a man went to inquire of God, he spoke thus: "Come, let us go to the seer"; for he who is now called a prophet was formerly called a seer.)

> [10] Then Saul said to his servant, "Well said; come, let us go." So they went to the city where the man of God was.

Saul goes from looking for donkeys to looking for the prophet; from hunting donkeys to desiring the word of the Lord.

It is interesting to note that it was Saul's servant that knew of Samuel (v.6). Saul seemed to be oblivious of Samuel the prophet and that he was in a nearby town. It was also wise of the servant, who not only thought of going to Samuel, but why they should go to Samuel, saying, *"perhaps he can show us the way that we should go."* As a matter of fact, it did not even seem as if Saul ever heard of Samuel, let alone knew of him. Saul knows Samuel merely as, "the man." Also, Saul is not prepared to go meet Samuel, having no gift to present to him. It appears as if the only knowledge that Saul has of Samuel is what his servant says of him.

The servant in this story shows more wisdom than the son of a well-known member of the community. The servant knows that Samuel the prophet could show them the way they should go. Wise servants today understand this truth.

Those with understanding will seek the direction that only the prophets can give them.

Each believer in Jesus has the ability to hear the voice of God for themselves; however, prophets can most often give clearer and deeper understanding and direction. Saul's servant appeared to understand this, while Saul seemed to be oblivious to this truth. It is sad, but many of our present leaders think that they do not need the input of others, including the prophetic voices around them. Think of what the church could become if we all utilized the gifts and ministries of the apostles, prophets, evangelists, pastors and teachers. What would the church look like if all five expressions of Jesus were alive and well in our churches?

It's important to remember, Saul came from a prominent family. 1 Samuel 9:1 tells us that Saul's father (Kish) was, "*a mighty man of power.*" Also, Samuel was the premier prophet and judge in Israel. Seeing that Samuel was very well known in Israel and that Saul's family was also very prominent, how is it that Saul never heard of Samuel? Saul, coming from a very prominent family in the region should have been better connected to the well-known and important people of Israel. Saul should have at least heard of Samuel, seeing that Samuel was the premier prophet of Israel. All the males of Israel would present themselves to the Lord three times a year. Saul and Samuel would have been in the same place worshipping God during the feasts. I find it odd that Saul seemed to know nothing of Samuel.

Saul already should have been well plugged in with the influential people of Israel. Even though Saul was the best Israel had to offer as a king, he was deficient in many areas, this being one of them.

Saul had nothing to present to Samuel as a gift. Saul's servant had one-fourth of a shekel of silver to show to Samuel and was willing to give it so the donkeys could be found.

By today's standards, one-fourth of a shekel of silver is about $2.50.

It is interesting that it was the servant that had this money, not the son of Kish, a mighty man of power. The servant was better prepared for this journey than the future King of Israel and son of a prominent businessman. The slave was better prepared in every way than was Saul.

Saul and the Servant

Saul	The Servant
Wanted to return home without the donkeys	Wanted to continue searching
Did not know of Samuel the Prophet	Knew of Samuel the Prophet
Did not prepare for the journey	Was better prepared for the journey
Did not have anything to bring as a gift to the prophet	Had one-fourth of a shekel of silver to bring to the prophet
Cared more for the immediate feelings of his father than for his financial stability	Cared about the financial status of his master
Did not care for his financial future and inheritance	Cared for the future financial stability of his master's family

After reading this and recognizing the wisdom shown by the servant you might ask, "Why did not God choose the servant to be the king instead of Saul?" The answer may lie in that the servant would never have been received by the people. We must remember that the people wanted someone that looked the part as much as was qualified for the part. The people wanted a king "like all the other nations." To have a servant arise and become the king would mean that these nations would ridicule Israel for generations to come. Saul was chosen because he had the inward potential along with the outward look of a king. Unfortunately, the inner potential of Saul was never fully developed, and the outward appearance was not enough to lead God's people.

It is unfortunate, but this story could be written about many church leaders today. Like Saul, many look good and pastoral on the outside, but the inward potential was never developed as it should have been. They look good in the suit but seem to be concerned with what people think of them, more than looking out for the future of the people of the church. Just as with a king, church leaders are required to make difficult decisions every day. Many of those decisions will have immediate consequences as well as long-term consequences. Far too many leaders look only at the immediate impact as they disregard the long-term effects.

I have known church leaders that got involved in building projects that they never should have. One church that I know of wanted to enlarge their building, add on a gymnasium with more classrooms, and remodel the existing sanctuary. The choice was made to secure a loan so that the work could be completed quickly instead of building as the money came in. Before the construction was finished the pastor felt called to another church and location, so he and his family left. This church leader left the church in the middle of a major building project.

As with most major transitions, like losing your pastor, this church lost many members. Many feel such insecurity when a pastor leaves the church that they leave as well. The abandonment experienced drives many from the church in these types of situations. Not only did this pastor leave the church with high debt and buildings only partially constructed, but his leaving left the people of the church feeling abandoned and insecure. This church went through several other pastors before the construction project was completed. In many churches and denominations pastors seem to come and go as if a revolving door is installed for them.

It is a sad day when church leaders become more interested in looking good before the people at the moment, but fail to prepare for the future. While this church was struggling to complete a building project, it was losing members because it was also going through pastors at a record rate. As a matter of fact, this church has had a new pastor every three to five years, except for two. Only two pastors remained more than five years in over 70 years of this church's existence. This is sad and quite pathetic!

Every one of these pastors was very Saul-like in character, in that they did not seem to care about the long-term effects their decisions were making. They did not appear to care that they were causing insecurity and feelings of abandonment in the people of the church, the people they were supposed to be serving. It seems their mindset was that having a new and bigger building would make them look good to the people and the denomination heads, so they got the church buried in debt. Oh, a bigger church in a better location has opened? So the pastor runs off to this new church, so it will look like he is doing something great for the denomination. Again, there is the not caring about the future of the people he is leaving behind.

It is extremely unfortunate, but this type of thing happens all the time in the church world today. Pastors and church leaders are often thinking more of themselves and the present moment, instead of being concerned with the future of the people they are supposed to be serving. We have these stories in the Bible so we can learn what to do, and what not to do. Pastors and church leaders will go to Bible College and Seminary, read countless books, read the Bible, and still do the 'what not to do'. This type of behavior is very Saul-like, causing us to be in need of a transition.

God was giving Israel just what they wanted in a king. Saul looked like an excellent candidate for the position of king, but as you can see he was not ready to lead a nation. It is sad to think that the servant was more qualified than Saul to be king. Often we are faced with the same dilemmas today. The associates are often more qualified to lead the church or organization than the present leader.

The question we must ask ourselves is: why is this so prevalent? Why are we drawn to those that have the look but not the character? If we are honest with ourselves, we often fall into the same trap as the Israelites. We may not say it with our mouth, but our actions say, "Now make us a king to judge us like all the nations (1 Samuel 8:5)." We may not verbalize it in this manner, but we are often driven by the same spirit and mentality as the people of Israel.

We want our church leaders to dress like a wealthy businessman or our favorite actor or actress. It is not uncommon for us to want a church leader with a particular style before we look at their credentials and ability to lead the church as he should. What is funny is that many want the pastor and his family to dress for success every Sunday and when they are out around town, while they receive pauper's pay. "We want you to live off 'mere change,' but you must look like a million bucks." No matter what end of the financial spectrum we may fall on, all of it is carnal at best.

We cannot afford to look merely at the surface, just because it looks like it is a quality that will produce what is needed. We need to look at the fruit of a person (or thing) before we make a judgment. This was true regarding the first King of Israel, and it is true regarding the spiritual leadership of today. We cannot afford to look through the lens of the flesh but through the lens of the Spirit. As we do this, we come under healthier leadership and coverings.

We all will be better off when we no longer want leaders like everyone else has, but we want the leader that God wants us to have.

1 Timothy 3:10

> *But let these also first be tested; then let them serve as deacons, being found blameless.*

> **Tested**–*to see whether a thing is genuine or not*

The Word of God is full of principles just like this one. Deacons are workers in the church, not necessarily leaders over the church. Since we are required to "test" deacons before they can work in the church, it is acceptable to do the same for other church leaders. The test is not about how good they look in the latest fashion, or how well they communicate, but in their overall character. It is not too much for us to expect our leaders to be "blameless" in all that they do. We can, and should, expect a high level of righteousness from those who lead the people of God.

When we are more concerned about a leader that merely dresses nice, and looks good in his position, and with leaders that care more about our immediate feelings than with our eternal home, we have actually done ourselves a disservice by coming under the leadership of a modern Saul.

All the things that were taking place with Saul in this story were a type of testing. It seems as if God wanted to refine and prove Saul. These events were exposing weaknesses in Saul that God was fully prepared to redeem. God wanted to strengthen the places where Saul was weak. It was now up to Saul to embrace what God was doing. If Saul had welcomed and engaged what God was doing, he would have been a great king and his throne would have been established. It is sad, but Saul failed to recognize what God was doing, causing him to not become the king that he otherwise could have been.

Chapter 5
Changed in an Instant

In the last chapter, we began to examine the life of Saul, Israel's first King. Saul appeared to be everything a king should be, but he still was lacking in some areas. As a matter of fact, Saul's servant seemed to be a better candidate for a king than Saul when compared together. However, God gave Israel just what they wanted in a king. Saul looked like an excellent candidate for the position of king, but as we have seen, he was not ready to lead a nation.

God's Answers to Saul's Shortcomings

1 Samuel 9:20-24

> [20] But as for your donkeys that were lost three days ago, do not be anxious about them, for they have been found. And on whom is all the desire of Israel? Is it not on you and on all your father's house?"

> [21] And Saul answered and said, "Am I not a Benjamite, of the smallest of the tribes of Israel, and my family the least of all the families of the tribe of Benjamin? Why then do you speak like this to me?"

> [22] Now Samuel took Saul and his servant and brought them into the hall, and had them sit in the place of honor among those who were invited; there were about thirty persons.

23 And Samuel said to the cook, "Bring the portion which I gave you, of which I said to you, 'Set it apart.' "

24 So the cook took up the thigh with its upper part and set it before Saul. And Samuel said, "Here it is, what was kept back. It was set apart for you. Eat; for until this time it has been kept for you since I said I invited the people." So Saul ate with Samuel that day.

From Being the Least
to a Place of Honor

After their initial introduction, Samuel invites Saul to a banquet. The first thing that Samuel says to Saul afterward is, "as for your donkeys that were lost three days ago, do not be anxious about them, for they have been found. *And on whom is all the desire of Israel? Is it not on you and on all your father's house?"* Samuel puts the heart of Saul at ease regarding his father's donkeys, then opens the door that leads to his being anointed as king (and commander) of Israel.

After the initial greeting and prophetic encounter, this is Saul's reaction to Samuel and his declaration, *"Am I not a Benjamite, of the smallest of the tribes of Israel, and my family the least of all the families of the tribe of Benjamin? Why then do you speak like this to me?"* Samuel declares the importance of Saul and his family only to have Saul state the opposite. It would be wise for us to ask some questions regarding Saul's response to Samuel's address. Is this humility or a low self-image? Is this true humility or is it false humility? Is this a strength or a weakness? A casual reading of this passage may lead us to think that Saul was merely caught off-guard and being humble. This is where many fail in their understanding of such things. Let us take a deeper look at Saul and his response.

Saul's Self-Image

While many will look at this and say that Saul was meek and humble, a deeper look reveals that he had a self-image problem. This is pride cloaked in false humility that shows a heart that is unsure of itself. Saul was not as humble as it seems in this story, and he had a difficult time receiving from the Lord through Samuel. This insecurity was a problem that manifested throughout Saul's reign as king. Most all of Saul's challenges and weaknesses can be traced to the insecurity and low self-image that he struggled with.

I know a church leader that God has called to be the apostolic father of his city and region, but because of his insecurities he has not been able to do much more than pastor a local church. Even though he is called and anointed to do much more than he is presently doing, he has not been able to affect the region as he is supposed to, out of fear of working with those outside of his church. It is unfortunate, but the only time he attends conferences and special meetings in his area are to look and see who from his church is at the meeting. He will literally reprimand the people of his church for attending these meetings as he rips into the church and ministry that hosted the event. This type of insecurity, manipulation, and control were present in the life and reign of Saul when he was king. It is grievous to think that an entire region is suffering because of the insecurity of the one that is supposed to be leading it spiritually. Think of all the people that are not receiving what they should be receiving because of this one that will not take the reins of his gifts and calling.

God has an answer to Saul's problem of low self-image and disbelief. Samuel invited Saul to a vital feast among very important people. Saul was given the best seat in the house (the seat of honor) and was given the best portion of food. It is as if God was trying to change the image Saul had of himself and his family. In one moment, a blink of the eye, Saul was the most important person in the nation. Before meeting Samuel and hearing the prophetic statement from the premier prophet of the land, Saul could get away with his self-image problem, but now he had to rise above his insecurities and the uncertainties they brought. Saul was about to be anointed King of Israel, but his mentality needed to catch up to this new reality.

As I write this, I am struck by the fact that some reading this book have been struggling in this same area. God has called you to do extraordinary things, but you are having a difficult time seeing yourself in the position that God says He created you for. It is time to overcome this weakness and be what God has called you to be. You have been waiting for the 'right thoughts and feelings,' but they will not come until you start doing what you are supposed to do. In other words, simply be what God has called you to be by doing what that calling requires. By doing this, the feelings and thoughts will catch up as you recognize the anointing and power of God at work through you.

A Private Meeting with the Prophet

1 Samuel 9:27

> *As they were going down to the outskirts of the city, Samuel said to Saul, "Tell the servant to go on ahead of us." And he went on. "But you stand here awhile, that I may announce to you the word of God."*

The end of chapter 9 shows us Samuel, the premier prophet of Israel, requesting a private meeting with Saul. In this private meeting with Samuel, God is providing what is needed for Saul to overcome his self-image problem. This meeting with Samuel should have shown Saul that more exists in him than he gives himself credit for. After reading this, I sat back and pondered this portion of the story and how God has done similar things for me over the years. Then I realized that God has done this countless time for numerous people, including you. If you have an identity problem, God has created encounters for you with the very people that can help you become what God has created you to be. Many of these encounters may not be with high-ranking spiritual leaders such as Samuel, but they are nonetheless what you needed to be shaped into the person God designed you to be. This portion of the story would be good to remember the next time you have a divine encounter with someone, or go through something that challenges what you believe about yourself.

Saul is Changed into Another Man

1 Samuel 10:1-16

[1] Then Samuel took a flask of oil and poured it on his head, and kissed him and said: "Is it not because the LORD has anointed you commander over His inheritance?

[2] When you have departed from me today, you will find two men by Rachel's tomb in the territory of Benjamin at Zelzah; and they will say to you, 'The donkeys which you went to look for have been found. And now your father has ceased caring about the donkeys and is worrying about you, saying, "What shall I do about my son?" '

[3] Then you shall go on forward from there and come to the terebinth tree of Tabor. There three men going up to God at Bethel will meet you, one carrying three young goats, another carrying three loaves of bread, and another carrying a skin of wine.

[4] And they will greet you and give you two loaves of bread, which you shall receive from their hands.

[5] After that, you shall come to the hill of God where the Philistine garrison is. And it will happen, when you have come there to the city, that you will meet a group of prophets coming down from the high place with a stringed instrument, a tambourine, a flute, and a harp before them; and they will be prophesying.

[6] Then the Spirit of the LORD will come upon you, and you will prophesy with them and be turned into another man.

[7] And let it be, when these signs come to you, that you do as the occasion demands; for God is with you.

⁸ *You shall go down before me to Gilgal, and surely I will come down to you to offer burnt offerings and make sacrifices of peace offerings. Seven days you shall wait, till I come to you and show you what you should do."*

⁹ *So it was when he had turned his back to go from Samuel, that God gave him another heart; and all those signs came to pass that day.*

¹⁰ *When they came there to the hill, there was a group of prophets to meet him; then the Spirit of God came upon him, and he prophesied among them.*

¹¹ *And it happened, when all who knew him formerly saw that he indeed prophesied among the prophets, that the people said to one another, "What is this that has come upon the son of Kish? Is Saul also among the prophets?"*

¹² *Then a man from there answered and said, "But who is their father?" Therefore it became a proverb: "Is Saul also among the prophets?"*

¹³ *And when he had finished prophesying, he went to the high place.*

¹⁴ *Then Saul's uncle said to him and his servant, "Where did you go?" So he said, "To look for the donkeys. When we saw that they were nowhere to be found, we went to Samuel."*

¹⁵ *And Saul's uncle said, "Tell me, please, what Samuel said to you."*

¹⁶ *So Saul said to his uncle, "He told us plainly that the donkeys had been found." But about the matter of the kingdom, he did not tell him what Samuel had said.*

Samuel anoints Saul to be commander over God's inheritance and gives him a prophetic word and instruction about what was going to take place to prove that this was the will of God and that he was truly going to be the first king of Israel. Samuel also prophesied saying, "the Spirit of the LORD will come upon you, and you will prophesy with them and be turned into another man." This all happened to Saul just as Samuel prophesied. Saul was changed in an instant and acted completely different than he did before. Just as we read, "when he had turned his back to go from Samuel, that God gave him another heart; and all those signs came to pass that day." God did all that He could do to make Saul into the man he needed to be to function as the king and leader he was created to be. Saul had a new heart and was completely changed.

This story is a prophetic picture of what happens in the life of the person that receives Jesus and is filled with His Spirit: he is entirely changed by God; he is given a new heart; and he is transformed into a new man. The principles of this story happen in the life of every man, woman, and child that accepts Jesus as Lord and Savior.

Recently I was moved by the Holy Spirit to put a trash can on the platform of my church, announcing that if anyone in the church struggled with such things as alcohol, drugs, cigarettes, pornography, etc. that God was calling them to repentance and He was present for deliverance. I proceeded to say that if those things were not presently in their car, then write the things they were repenting of on a piece of paper and throw it into the trash can. No one seemed to move and take advantage of the moment until I began rebuking these things and those struggling with them, saying, "You have been saved through faith in Jesus and washed in His blood. You have been filled with His Holy Spirit. You now have all the power of Heaven at your disposal. Do not tell me you cannot overcome these problems! Do not say you are not strong enough to be freed from these strongholds! To say that you cannot be free from this thing is a slap in the face of Jesus Who gave His life so that you could be free! You are now filled with the power of Heaven! Repent and be FREE!" At this point, several came up and repented and were set free.

Whether it be Saul or the church leader today, it is unacceptable to continue holding onto the things that keep us from being able to be all that God has called us to be. It is a slap in the face of Jesus, who gave everything so that we could be free and empowered to serve Him, fulfilling the call upon our life. We have got to stop making excuses for our powerlessness and be the man or woman that God has called us to be.

I want to offer this challenge to everyone that reads this. The challenge is simply this, NO MORE EXCUSES! To be honest with ourselves would mean we would agree that we simply make up too many excuses for not doing what is supposed to be done, and for not being what God meant for us to be.

It is time to rise above the excuses of yesterday and start believing what God has spoken to us. Only then can we become what God has said of us. There are gifts and callings lying dormant in nearly everyone reading this right now. It is time to awaken those gifts, answer the call, and fulfill the Word of God for your life. The world is waiting for you to become all that you are supposed to become. NO MORE EXCUSES!

It ALL Happened Just as Samuel Prophesied

An important thing for us to understand is found in 1 Samuel 10:9,

"So it was when he had turned his back to go from Samuel, that God gave him another heart; and all those signs came to pass that day."

This is probably the most important verse in this passage. *"God gave Saul another heart"*. This shows that no matter what else was going on within Saul, he surely had the capacity for change. Every shortcoming in Saul was answered in this one verse. That is why no excuses were suitable for Saul. He had everything that he needed to fulfill this new position of king over Israel. This principle is the same with you and me today.

When we come to Jesus, we are given a new heart as we are filled with the Holy Spirit. Every Spirit-filled believer has the power and strength to overcome every obstacle in the process of becoming everything that God has called them to be. Saul had the ability to be a great king. Even in areas he lacked, God gave him everything he would need to fulfill the call on his life. Saul had no reason for not rising to the occasion afforded him.

I do not want to keep harping on this, but it is absolutely critical that we get this concept. Way too many in the body of Christ today are living far below their calling, and because of this, they are not producing the quantity or quality of fruit as they should. It is a sad truth, but it is a truth nonetheless. God wants every one of us to be walking in the power of the Spirit every day, and all day. The life I am describing is not a life for a select few, but for everyone that has accepted Jesus as Lord. We are to look more like Jesus every day. Looking like Jesus means we are to walk like Him, talk like Him, think like Him, act like him, heal like Him, work miracles like Him, etc. Your life should look more like a life found in the pages of scripture than a life found in a popular magazine.

Many are called to evangelize through acts of power, but have made excuses as to why they cannot go out and minister to strangers. Some have a call to healing ministry. Many are waiting for someone to come with the power to set them free from their sickness and disease, but excuses are being made and lies believed, so that gift is lying dormant. Some apostles and prophets have been called to revolutionize the church, but because of the present church structure and the excuses they have made, the church remains in shallow waters. Others are called to be apostles and prophets that will unleash the power of heaven into the church, but are floundering around as they struggle with feeling worthy of their call. The excuses they have made have kept them from walking in power on a level that would otherwise change the dynamics of entire regions. What prevents them from fulfilling the call of God on their life? Simply put, Excuses!

I am passionate about this because I realize that until we all become what we have been called to be, and do what we are called to do, the church will continue to lack power and significance. There will be a great void that will continue, thus, where you find a shortage in the church, it is not only the church that suffers. The world will suffer as well, because the problems in our culture and society will not be met by those who should have the answers.

The righteous will never rise to the place of prominence in our culture if we keep making excuses.

If we remain in the low place that our explanations create for us we will never be recognized as the problem solvers we are designed to be. This is true for us today, as it was for Saul in his time.

Everything that was prophesied to Saul happened just as Samuel had said. This is an excellent passage of scripture that shows just how much God was interested and willing to make Saul the BEST KING that he could be. God had invested much into Saul and his future. The nation was at stake so God held nothing back, as we can see from our story.

When God calls someone, He gives them everything they need to fulfill the function He calls them to. It was up to Saul to take what God had given Him and make something of it. Saul had some choices to make about himself and his future. He could take what was given to him and become the best king Israel would ever have, or he could reject what was given to him and remain the same. Rejecting what God had given him would mean that Saul would face every problem that he had from that point on with the same low self-image and the same insecurities he had struggled with for most of his life. Remember, the same choices are given to you and me.

We will either choose to accept all that God has given to us, or we will reject it.

Rejecting God's provision will mean no real change, but taking what God has provided will mean great power for the road ahead.

1 Samuel 10:5-6

[5] After that, you shall come to the hill of God where the Philistine garrison is. And it will happen, when you have come

there to the city, that you will meet a group of prophets coming down from the high place with a stringed instrument, a tambourine, a flute, and a harp before them; and they will be prophesying.

6 Then the Spirit of the LORD will come upon you, and you will prophesy with them and be turned into another man.

When Saul met the prophets and prophesied among them, he was changed into another man. Saul was then a new man with a new heart. Saul needed the prophets to help him get where he needed to be. It began with the prophetic ministry of Samuel, then was followed through by this company of prophets that he met coming down from the high places. All throughout the Bible we find the importance of the ministry of the prophets, but today in many churches the prophets and their ministry have been rejected. If you asked most Christians today, "do you have prophets in your church?", most Christians would shrink from such a question, and yet the ministry of the prophet is so valuable that Jesus Himself was known and recognized as a prophet.

1 Samuel 10:13

And when he had finished prophesying, he went to the high place.

After prophesying with the prophets, Saul goes to the high place. The high places were places of worship and communion with God. This shows the heart of Saul, at this point, is towards God. He is a new man with a new heart, carrying the anointing of the prophets, and now he is in the place of worship and communion with God.

This did not happen until Saul had the word of the Lord from Samuel, and after he had met the prophets coming from the high places. This is a compelling and telling story about how those of us today are to grow into the fullness of who we were created to be. This is not a story of how God used to move, but how God still moves. We need the prophets today just as much as Saul needed them during his time. God uses His instruments, the prophets, to bring great and powerful change into our lives. It is unfortunate when the prophets are shut down by unbelieving church leaders. When this happens, the people of God cannot experience all that God has for them.

Leaving His High Place

1 Samuel 10:14-16

> [14] Then Saul's uncle said to him and his servant, "Where did you go?" So he said, "To look for the donkeys. When we saw that they were nowhere to be found, we went to Samuel."
>
> [15] And Saul's uncle said, "Tell me, please, what Samuel said to you."
>
> [16] So Saul said to his uncle, "He told us plainly that the donkeys had been found." But about the matter of the kingdom, he did not tell him what Samuel had said.

It is not clear when or where Saul meets his uncle, but his uncle asks him about his journey. He only asked, "Where did you go?" Saul explains how they went to see Samuel. Saul also speaks of Samuel as if he now knows him very well. When he and his servant were looking for the donkeys, Saul did not have any idea who Samuel was, but now Saul begins a long relationship with Samuel. Saul's uncle wants to hear all that Samuel said to Saul, but Saul tells him nothing other than the portion about the donkeys. It is written, "But about the matter of the kingdom, he did not tell him what Samuel had said." The most important part of his meeting with Samuel he leaves out.

After all that God did for Saul to change him from the inside, and to give him a new heart and to change him into a new man, Saul leaves out the most important aspects of the story. Saul was anointed by Samuel as commander of God's inheritance, and he fails to tell his uncle about this. As you can see, Saul had a choice about how he was going to respond to his uncle's question, and he chose to revert to his insecurities and low self-image. This is the challenge each of us must overcome in our walk with the Lord. We must never give in to the dangers of yesterday, or the false self-image that God delivered us from. We must hold onto what God speaks to us now. Our yesterdays are over.

It is unfortunate, but Saul left the place of intimacy and communion with God. It is as if he forgot everything that just happened to him before going into the high places of worship, intimacy, and communion. It was only by remaining in the high place with God that Saul would have been secure in who he was as God made him. Coming down from the high place put Saul right back where he began. It is the same for you and me today. When God speaks to our true self and character, we are to remain close to Him. It is only while in real communion and intimacy with the Father that we can stay in the fullness of His declaration over us.

When God asks something of you and me, we are not allowed to have a low self-image of ourselves, nor are we allowed to see ourselves other than what God has said about us. The times when we have an experience with God, the blessing is not merely for the moment, but to change us for our future. Blessings may be an answer for the moment, but they are also sent to change our heart and change us into another man. Even if we struggle with our self-image, God will make way for us to have a new heart and to become a new man (or woman). He will give us everything we need to fulfill what He is asking of us. Our job is to assimilate everything He is giving us, allowing the change to be full and complete, and we do this by remaining in the high place with Him.

Chapter 6
The Challenge of Kings

When God asks something of us, we are not allowed to make excuses as to why we cannot do what He is asking. We are not allowed to have a low self-image of ourselves, nor are we allowed to see ourselves other than how God sees us. And we are never allowed to use a low self-image as an excuse to not do as God asks. Remember that God knows everything about you. If He asks you to do something, it is because He knows you are capable of accomplishing the task.

The times when God blesses us is not merely for the moment, but to change us for our future. Blessings bring an answer for the moment, but they are also sent to change our heart and change us into another man, and these changes are to be a life change that endures forever.

Even if we struggle with our self-image, God will make way for us to have a new heart and to become a new man (or woman). He will give us everything we need to fulfill what He is asking of us. Our job is to assimilate into our heart and life everything He is giving us, allowing the change to be full and complete (from Chapter 5).

These are some of the lessons we learn from looking at Saul. Saul was chosen by God to lead His people, but he lacked in the areas of his self-image and self-worth. God gave Saul everything he needed to overcome these weaknesses, but he continued to hold onto an image of himself that held him down and caused him to make bad decisions.

A Failed King

1 Samuel 15:1-35

> [1] *Samuel also said to Saul, "The LORD sent me to anoint you king over His people, over Israel. Now, therefore, heed the voice of the words of the LORD.*

Here we find Saul being instructed to "heed the voice of the words of the LORD." This story begins with a simple instruction to 'do what God commands you to do!' If we are going to do anything of any real value for God and His Kingdom, then we, too, must do what God commands us to do. As the king over God's people, Saul was expected to be obedient to the LORD in all things.

> [2] *Thus says the LORD of hosts: 'I will punish Amalek for what he did to Israel, how he ambushed him on the way when he came up from Egypt.'*
>
> [3] *Now go and attack Amalek, and utterly destroy all that they have, and do not spare them, but kill both man and woman, infant and nursing child, ox and sheep, camel and donkey.'"*

As brutal as this may seem, God expected Saul to carry out this command to its fullest. The Amalekites were to be completely destroyed for what they did to God's people. As we can plainly see, the command was clear and concise: destroy all that they have, including the people.

> *4 So Saul gathered the people together and numbered them in Telaim, two hundred thousand foot soldiers and ten thousand men of Judah.*
>
> *5 And Saul came to a city of Amalek and lay in wait in the valley.*
>
> *6 Then Saul said to the Kenites, "Go, depart, get down from among the Amalekites, lest I destroy you with them. For you showed kindness to all the children of Israel when they came up out of Egypt." So the Kenites departed from among the Amalekites.*

Saul shows kindness to the Kenites. This was a good thing that God would honor. Just as the Amalekites were to be destroyed because of how they treated Israel, the Kenites could be spared because of the way they helped Israel.

> *7 And Saul attacked the Amalekites, from Havilah all the way to Shur, which is east of Egypt.*
>
> *8 He also took Agag king of the Amalekites alive and utterly destroyed all the people with the edge of the sword.*
>
> *9 But Saul and the people spared Agag and the best of the sheep, the oxen, the fatlings, the lambs, and all that was good, and were unwilling to utterly destroy them. But everything despised and worthless, that they utterly destroyed.*

Here we find Saul carrying out the command of the LORD, but only partially. God said, *"Now go and attack Amalek, and utterly destroy all that they have, and do not spare them, but kill both man and woman, infant and nursing child, ox and sheep, camel and donkey (v.2)."* Saul and the army of Israel were to completely annihilate the Amalekites, but we see that he spared the king and the best things in the city.

Notice that other than King Agag, Saul did not save the people; however, he spared the best of the animals "and all that was good." This shows where Saul's heart was. He did not have pity for the people, but he spared the animals that he wanted to save for himself and the people of Israel.

How many leaders, pastors, business owners, etc. do things similar to this? It seems that some are more concerned about their own reputation, the building they meet in, and what they look like on TV, more than the people they are to have a heart for. It is an unfortunate truth, but many in ministry would sacrifice others in their care before they would sacrifice their own reputations.

It is sad but true, the spirit of Saul is alive today, and it is found in the church.

10 Now the word of the LORD came to Samuel, saying,

11 "I greatly regret that I have set up Saul as king, for he has turned back from following Me, and has not performed My commandments." And it grieved Samuel, and he cried out to the LORD all night.

When God raised up Saul to be king, He expected him to be obedient to the commands He gave him. When the king (or someone that are over people) is disobedient to the LORD and refuses to do what God has instructed, He will regret allowing that one to be over the people He loves. It does not matter if it is a king of the Old Testament or a pastor in the modern church, we are to be fully obedient to the LORD and do everything He asks of us. I, personally, never want to hear God say that He regrets setting me up as a church leader. I for one want to be obedient to the Lord in all things and everything He asks of me.

12 So when Samuel rose early in the morning to meet Saul, it was told Samuel, saying, "Saul went to Carmel, and indeed, he set up a monument for himself; and he has gone on around, passed by, and gone down to Gilgal."

This is a fascinating verse. This shows just how detached Saul was from God and His will. While God is telling Samuel that He regretted making Saul king, Saul was building monuments to himself. Saul saw his campaign against the Amalekites as a complete victory, but God saw it as a failure.

Often church leaders fall into this trap without giving it a second thought. Churches exist all over the globe that promote the pastor more than they promote Jesus. These are men and women that are too busy building monuments to their own glory when they should be exalting the name of Jesus and His word instead of themselves.

It is also better to get God's perspective on things before we declare victory or failure. Often we think we are doing fine, but in reality, we are missing the mark with God. Our goal should be to hear the voice of the Lord declare, *"Well done, good and faithful servant..." (Matthew 25:21).* Instead of declaring it over ourselves and our own work, we should wait to build our monuments until God says, "well done"; then the monument should be erected in His name alone.

Here in my own home town, we have many small churches. It seems as if a new church pops up almost every week. One of the things that I have noticed about many of these churches is that they appear to be no more than "monuments" erected to their founders. I have driven by some of these churches that have built large banners with the church leader's face and name as big as day, but the only mention of Jesus might be somewhere in the name of the church. Many have "Pastor Appreciation" events, which are not entirely wrong, but I have yet to see "Jesus Appreciation" events in these places. In other words, many of our churches today are built on the carnality of another that exalts man more than God. As I wrote a few lines prior, the spirit of Saul is alive today.

> [13] *Then Samuel went to Saul, and Saul said to him, "Blessed are you of the LORD! I have performed the commandment of the LORD."*

Half obedience is still disobedience.

When God gives us a command, we are to follow the command to its fullest and do it completely. As this story so clearly shows, Saul was only partially obedient to the instructions of the Lord. Saul's arrogance must have turned Samuel's stomach at this point.

> [14] *But Samuel said, "What then is this bleating of the sheep in my ears, and the lowing of the oxen which I hear?"*

We may think that we can get away with being less than obedient, but God always knows the truth about us and the truth will always be revealed. Saul was about to continue his self-exalting brag session with Samuel, but Samuel cuts it off.

> [15] *And Saul said, "They have brought them from the Amalekites; for the people spared the best of the sheep and the oxen, to sacrifice to the LORD your God; and the rest we have utterly destroyed."*

Now the excuses begin. Notice how Saul tries to 'spiritualize' his disobedience? He starts by blaming the people and saying, "the people spared the best of the sheep and the oxen, to sacrifice to the LORD your God..." This is carnal human behavior. We do not want to take responsibility for our actions and failures, so we blame someone else. This type of blame shifting began in the garden after the fall. After Adam and Eve had eaten the forbidden fruit and God came to meet them in the garden, God asked Adam why they ate the fruit He told them was off limits. Adams reply, *"The woman whom You gave to be with me, she gave me of the tree, and I ate (Genesis 3:12)."* Not only did Adam pass blame, but he passed blame to God. Most people may not go so far as to blame God, but most of us struggle with shifting blame just as Adam and Saul did. Saul had the chance at this point to repent and come clean. Instead, he begins throwing out excuses as to why it was not his fault for his disobedience.

"It was the people, they did it! They made me!"

16 Then Samuel said to Saul, "Be quiet! And I will tell you what the LORD said to me last night." And he said to him, "Speak on."

17 So Samuel said, "When you were little in your own eyes, were you not the head of the tribes of Israel? And did not the LORD anoint you king over Israel?

18 Now the LORD sent you on a mission, and said, 'Go, and utterly destroy the sinners, the Amalekites, and fight against them until they are consumed.'

19 Why then did you not obey the voice of the LORD? Why did you swoop down on the spoil, and do evil in the sight of the LORD?"

Samuel says to Saul, "Be quiet!" Samuel says this to the king, the one that could take his head off his shoulders. The boldness of the prophet is recognized for his unwavering commitment and obedience to the Lord. When we treat the command of the LORD with contempt by being disobedient to the LORD, causing our spiritual fathers to respond to us as Samuel did with Saul, this shows that we have fallen to very low levels. When Samuel tells Saul to "be quiet" I believe it was out of frustration and mercy. Frustration because of the failure of Saul that now reflects on Samuel, but also mercy because Saul was digging a deeper hole for himself with his excuse making.

Leaders are not allowed to make excuses, blaming the people under them for their failures. Leaders are to be just as that title implies, a LEADER! By blaming the people under him, Saul was forfeiting his authority as king and giving it over to the people. Church leaders do this each time they blame the people around them for their failures. When we blame the people of our churches for our failures, we have given our authority over to those we continue to blame. We must remember that the people do the things they do while under our leadership. If the people fail and continually do things out of alignment with our will and desire, we must take responsibility, since they are doing these things while under our leadership. The people found it easy to be disobedient to the command of the Lord by sparing the best livestock because they witnessed their king spare Agag, king of the Amalekites.

> [20] And Saul said to Samuel, "But I have obeyed the voice of the LORD, and gone on the mission on which the LORD sent me, and brought back Agag king of Amalek; I have utterly destroyed the Amalekites.
>
> [21] But the people took of the plunder, sheep, and oxen, the best of the things which should have been utterly destroyed, to sacrifice to the LORD your God in Gilgal."

Saul knew what God had commanded him. He was to destroy everything and everyone. He was not to keep King Agag alive, nor was he to keep any of the animals alive. Everything was to be destroyed! This point needs to be made again:

> *Partial obedience is not obedience,*
> *especially when we know exactly*
> *what we are supposed to be doing.*

Saul tries to tell Samuel that the best animals were kept alive so that they could sacrifice them to the LORD, but God NEVER asked for this!

> *[22] So Samuel said: "Has the LORD as great delight in burnt offerings and sacrifices, as in obeying the voice of the LORD? Behold, to obey is better than sacrifice, and to heed than the fat of rams.*
>
> *[23] For rebellion is as the sin of witchcraft, and stubbornness is as iniquity and idolatry. Because you have rejected the word of the LORD, He also has rejected you from being king."*

God is far more interested in our obedience than our sacrifice. The ONLY sacrifice that God is pleased with is the sacrifice that comes from our obedience. Saul tries to spiritualize his disobedience to the Lord's command. This, unfortunately, happens quite often. Leaders make mistakes by not being fully obedient to God, then trying to explain it away, attempting to make their failures into something spiritual. Disobedience can NEVER be changed into something holy and acceptable to God, no matter how hard we try or how cunning our excuses are, disobedience will always be disobedience and a sin before God.

Disobedience to the command of the LORD
is rebellion, and rebellion is witchcraft.

Stubbornness (doing things our own way) is as iniquity (lawlessness) and idolatry. When we put our own will above God's will we make ourselves our own god.

Who you obey is your god.

Obey the commands of the LORD, and He is
your God; follow your own heart and lusts,
and you have become your own god.

When we understand this, we see that idolatry is very much alive in our churches and culture. I feel as if I am repeating myself too much, but the point needs to be driven home.

Partial obedience is not obedience at all.

When we do things our way instead of God's way we are engaged in witchcraft. This is no small thing. God wants our complete obedience. Anything less is a sin.

> *24 Then Saul said to Samuel, "I have sinned, for I have transgressed the commandment of the LORD and your words because I feared the people and obeyed their voice.*
>
> *25 Now, therefore, please pardon my sin, and return with me, that I may worship the LORD."*

Saul admits his guilt and admits that he "transgressed the command of the LORD." Why did Saul disobey God? He "feared the people and obeyed their voice." Remember that Saul wanted to return home after three days of searching for his father's donkeys because he feared that his father would become worried about him being gone so long. Saul worried too much about what people thought of him.

In this story, he admits that he "feared the people" so he obeyed them as if they were in control. The king of God's people gave over his authority and rule to the people he was supposed to be leading. By his actions and choices, Saul showed that he still carried a low self-image of himself and that he held the people in higher regard than the Lord and His commands.

> [26] But Samuel said to Saul, "I will not return with you, for you have rejected the word of the LORD, and the LORD has rejected you from being king over Israel."
>
> [27] And as Samuel turned around to go away, Saul seized the edge of his robe, and it tore.
>
> [28] So Samuel said to him, "The LORD has torn the kingdom of Israel from you today, and has given it to a neighbor of yours, who is better than you.
>
> [29] And also the strength of Israel will not lie nor relent. For He is not a man, that He should relent."

Because of his disobedience, God rejected Saul as king and found someone else to replace him. Samuel told Saul that God found someone *"who is better than you."* Samuel pulled no punches here. Saul was rejected by God, and Samuel informed him that God had chosen someone better than him. Can you image hearing these words from the premier prophet of the land? The thought of being rejected by God and replaced with someone "who is better than you" should be a wake-up call to those of us in ministry. We are not as indispensable as we think. If we are disobedient to the LORD and continue in that disobedience, we could be replaced as easily as Saul was. It is regrettable, but we are watching this today. Many in church leadership are being replaced by those "better than" them. God is cleaning the church by clearing out failed and weak leadership. The Sauls must go.

> [30] *Then he said, "I have sinned; yet honor me now, please, before the elders of my people and before Israel, and return with me, that I may worship the LORD your God."*

> [31] *So Samuel turned back after Saul, and Saul worshiped the LORD.*

Instead of repenting and begging God and Samuel for forgiveness, Saul wanted Samuel to accompany him so that he looked good to the people. Just after he was told that God rejected him as king, Saul still refused to truly repent and turn from his arrogance and disobedience, and once again put the people before God. How could this man be so arrogant and hardened of heart?

> [32] *Then Samuel said, "Bring Agag king of the Amalekites here to me." So Agag came to him cautiously. And Agag said, "Surely the bitterness of death is past."*

> [33] *But Samuel said, "As your sword has made women childless, so shall your mother be childless among women." And Samuel hacked Agag in pieces before the LORD in Gilgal.*

Samuel the Prophet finished the job that the king refused to do.

It is an embarrassment when a person in a leadership position has someone in a lesser position come to do the job that they could not do. Saul proved himself a failure as king when he failed to do what was expected of him as king. The prophet had to step into the position of the king (so to speak) to fulfill the command of the LORD. Saul lost his position as king because of his disobedience. It is as if God said, "Since you refuse to act like the king, you no longer need the anointing of the king."

This happens around us all the time. Remember Saul's servant? He was more prepared than Saul was when looking for the donkeys and then for Samuel. Here in this story, Samuel the prophet was more willing to carry out the command given to the king than the king himself.

> [34] *Then Samuel went to Ramah, and Saul went up to his house at Gibeah of Saul.*
>
> [35] *And Samuel went no more to see Saul until the day of his death. Nevertheless, Samuel mourned for Saul, and the LORD regretted that He had made Saul king over Israel.*

Not only did Saul lose his position as king (in regard to God), he also lost the friendship of Samuel and the prophetic input that Samuel provided. Saul fell to a very low place because of his disobedience to the command of the LORD.

This story provides a picture for those who have been in rebellion similar to the rebellion of Saul, and those associated with the disobedient leader. The Sauls of our day need to repent, while the Samuels of our day need to stop coddling those in disobedience.

The time comes when we need to cut off and step out of the lives of those in willful violation.

In my life time I have seen many 'big names' fall into immorality — usually affairs and divorce. I have also watched as other 'big names' come to the side of those who have fallen. At first it looks good, as if these ones are going to restore the fallen brother, but unfortunately this is often not the case. These restoration sessions often turn into a type of photo op for those wanting to use the name of the fallen to expand their own name and ministry. Often after a time of 'restoration' the fallen brother goes and does something just as heinous as the first offense, revealing that no genuine repentance and restoration was present at all. Of course, this is not always what happens, but unfortunately, this is frequently the case.

It is time that we move and operate as Samuel did. If the fallen truly repent then we must do all that we can to restore them. For those who refuse to repent, we need to step away from them and cut ourselves off from them as Samuel did with Saul. In our wishy-washy 'greasy grace' world, this goes against what many are preaching, but it is nonetheless Biblical and right.

1 Corinthians 5:9-11

[9] *I wrote to you in my epistle not to keep company with sexually immoral people.*

[10] *Yet I certainly did not mean with the sexually immoral people of this world, or with the covetous, or extortioners, or idolaters, since then you would need to go out of the world.*

[11] *But now I have written to you not to keep company with anyone named a brother, who is sexually immoral, or covetous, or an idolater, or a reviler, or a drunkard, or an extortioner – not even to eat with such a person.*

I do not see how this could get any clearer.

We are to cut off those who claim to be Christians, but refuse to repent and live righteously – NOT LIKE THE WORLD!

We are not even to be eating with a brother that is in willful sin and disobedience to Christ. I am not sure why this is so hard for us to understand, but many have difficulty comprehending this principle.

Our hearts should always be about reconciliation, but some in the church refuse to repent when they fall into sin. Just as Samuel walked away from Saul, we need to learn to walk away from the willfully disobedient around us. Again, not those who do not know Christ, but those who claim Christ and still are in intentional and conscious sin and disobedience. We need to step away from them, allowing God to deal with them as He sees fit.

Regardless of your title or position,
God expects you to be fully obedient to him.
No one is exempt from this truth.

Obedience to God and His word is not a suggestion but a command. Saul fell from grace and was found severely wanting in his relationship with God and as king over God's people. His disobedience caused God to regret making him king and led to him being replaced by someone better. God's patience ran out, and Saul lost everything.

Have you noticed that God is not impressed with titles? God is not impressed with the crowns on our heads or the degrees on our walls. God is impressed with our obedience to him.

In this transition that we are in, God is raising up those who will be obedient to Him in all things. Those being brought low and being replaced are those who reject God by being disobedient to His commands.

If you want to be recognized and used by God for His glory, it begins and ends with obedience.

Chapter 7
Becoming Kings

It is sometimes hard to make the transitions needed to put us where we need to be for a fresh and 'right now' move of God, but change we must. It is a bit funny, but for the most part, we are only transitioning back to God's Word and God's will – nothing more. God is expecting us to come fully back to Him and to obey what He has put in His eternal word. This may sound strange, but as we have been finding, we have been separated from God in many ways because we have not been living wholly by His Word. The transition is here as it was at the time of Saul and David.

1 Samuel 15:34-35

34 Then Samuel went to Ramah, and Saul went up to his house at Gibeah of Saul.

35 And Samuel went no more to see Saul until the day of his death. Nevertheless, Samuel mourned for Saul, and the LORD regretted that He had made Saul king over Israel.

Saul was not only disobedient to the will of God, but he also was disrespectful towards Samuel, the premier prophet of Israel. Although Saul was the king (a political figure), Samuel was the spiritual leader of Israel. He deserved respect and honor even from the king, and yet Saul was so caught up in his personal glory that he found it easy to disrespect the one responsible for setting him in position as king.

In the modern church today, we have a strange array of ideas and expressions towards those in a position of authority. I know church leaders that demand the people of their church to treat them in such a manner that it looks more like a servant-master relationship than a shepherd-lamb relationship. I have seen disgusting displays of abuse of authority from church leaders that act as if the only purpose of the people of the church is to serve them. This type of behavior is usually wrapped in such titles as 'Armor Bearer'. These real biblical concepts and ideologies are being perverted to benefit the church leader and not the members of the congregation.

I have also witnessed the pendulum swing to the other extreme. I know church leaders that do almost everything in the church with very little help from anyone in the congregation.

Both extremes are wrong. To act as if the people are your servants, doing nothing but speaking from the pulpit is entirely wrong. However, it is equally wrong for church leaders to do everything in the church. Somewhere a healthy balance exists. Somewhere real leadership is setting the example of doing the work of ministry and delegating it others.

Remember, we are to establish the example
for others to follow.

This means that church leaders are to roll up their sleeves and get dirty, and we should be doing it alongside others that are willing to do the same. Pastor, when was the last time you vacuumed the church or scrubbed a toilet?

The New King of Israel

1 Samuel 16:1-5

> [1] *Now the LORD said to Samuel, "How long will you mourn for Saul, seeing I have rejected him from reigning over Israel? Fill your horn with oil, and go; I am sending you to Jesse the Bethlehemite. For I have provided Myself a king among his sons."*
>
> [2] *And Samuel said, "How can I go? If Saul hears it, he will kill me." But the LORD said, "Take a heifer with you, and say, 'I have come to sacrifice to the LORD.'*
>
> [3] *Then invite Jesse to the sacrifice, and I will show you what you shall do; you shall anoint for Me the one I name to you."*
>
> [4] *So Samuel did what the LORD said, and went to Bethlehem. And the elders of the town trembled at his coming, and said, "Do you come peaceably?"*
>
> [5] *And he said, "Peaceably; I have come to sacrifice to the LORD. Sanctify yourselves, and come with me to the sacrifice." Then he consecrated Jesse and his sons and invited them to the sacrifice.*

And Samuel STILL mourned for Saul! Why? Samuel poured himself into Saul, making him a type of spiritual father to Saul. Now his spiritual son has fallen and become a threat to him and has been rejected by God. Samuel's mourning for Saul shows the heart and character of Samuel. If Saul had the same character, he may have mourned over his sin and disobedience, which would have changed this story and his destiny completely.

***A demand is placed on those in leadership–
a need to respect and honor one another;***

but especially our fathers and mothers in the faith. We are to revere those who have poured themselves into us.

I cannot tell you how many times I have seen people mistreat and neglect those who helped to raise them up in the things of the Spirit. This is especially true when someone makes it into the big leagues of ministry (so to speak).

I have watched where the Samuels of our day pour themselves into their spiritual sons and daughters only to be left by the side of the road when those sons and daughters make it. It is not always fame and fortune or the big ministry. It can be almost anything that detracts the sons from their fathers.

This has happened to me many times. People come into my church and when I see great potential in them, I develop a relationship with them and pour myself into them, raising them up much the same way Jesus raised up His disciples. After months, (sometimes years) and countless hours, they disappear without as much as a proper goodbye. These types of Sauls cut themselves off and stunt their own growth by walking away from the source of influence and empowering God established in their life. In nearly every one of these circumstances, they move on to nothing. They have to start all over because they left the one that was raising them up as a son or daughter in the Lord.

Several years ago a family came to the church and became members. I saw and recognized the potential for ministry in the husband and wife, so my wife and I developed a close relationship with them (or so we thought). For years we poured into them and steadily escorted them up the ladder of ministry. I had a plan to make them the associate pastors of the church with the idea of turning the church over to them. Literally just before I was to establish them as my associate pastors, they disappeared without saying goodbye. It took me weeks to track them down and speak to them. No real reason was given for leaving the church and ministry; they simply wanted to move on. They never knew just how close they were to being asked to be the associate pastors of the church which would have directly led to being the senior pastors of the church. It is sad, but their disrespect and dishonor kept them from gaining the entire church.

This, unfortunately, is not an isolated story. Similar things have happened throughout my ministry, and many other church leaders have gone through the same thing. The Samuels have been pouring themselves out for others, and the Sauls treat it as if it is without value. These Sauls never seem to realize that it is the Samuels in their life that makes it possible for them to be in the position they are in. This has got to change. The church will not grow as it should until this is resolved. Fathers in the faith are to rise up sons and daughters that will, in turn, take the given inheritance and cause it to grow and multiply. This is to be done as the sons and daughters honor their spiritual fathers and mothers. Once dishonor creeps in much of the inheritance is lost.

It is interesting to note that when Samuel came to Bethlehem, the elders of the city became afraid, asking, *"Do you come peaceably (v.5)?"* The elders of Bethlehem knew that a prophet such as Samuel would not come for merely a visit. A prophet on the level of Samuel would come either to bless or to curse. This is why they approached Samuel with great reverence and even fear; in other words, that treated him with genuine respect and honor, the respect and honor due his position.

The elders of Bethlehem gave the respect and honor to Samuel that Saul also should have given. Samuel was not some out of line parking lot prophet, or a house prophet, but the premier prophet of Israel. The king himself should have honored Samuel as God's mouthpiece to the nation. These elders knew that Samuel carried with him the word of the Lord that could build and establish or tear down and destroy. When Saul was looking for his father's donkeys, he did not even know who Samuel was. Compare the way Saul treated Samuel to the way these city elders treat Samuel when he arrives.

Samuel came to Bethlehem to find the man that would replace Saul as king. Samuel was in for somewhat of a surprise and education in the way God looks at people. God is so much higher than you and I that it should never shock us that God thinks on a much higher level as well. He sees what we cannot see and knows what is unknowable to you and I. Samuel found this to be true.

Not Important Enough
to be Invited to the Party

1 Samuel 16:6-13

> *6 So it was, when they came, that he looked at Eliab and said, "Surely the LORD's anointed is before Him!"*

> *7 But the LORD said to Samuel, "Do not look at his appearance or at his physical stature because I have refused him. For the LORD does not see as man sees; for man looks at the outward appearance, but the LORD looks at the heart."*

> *8 So Jesse called Abinadab and made him pass before Samuel. And he said, "Neither has the LORD chosen this one."*

⁹ *Then Jesse made Shammah pass by. And he said, "Neither has the LORD chosen this one."*

¹⁰ *Thus Jesse made seven of his sons pass before Samuel. And Samuel said to Jesse, "The LORD has not chosen these."*

¹¹ *And Samuel said to Jesse, "Are all the young men here?" Then he said, "There remains yet the youngest, and there he is, keeping the sheep." And Samuel said to Jesse, "Send and bring him. For we will not sit down till he comes here."*

¹² *So he sent and brought him in. Now he was ruddy, with bright eyes, and good-looking. And the LORD said, "Arise, anoint him; for this is the one!"*

¹³ *Then Samuel took the horn of oil and anointed him in the midst of his brothers, and the Spirit of the LORD came upon David from that day forward. So Samuel arose and went to Ramah.*

Samuel is now with Jesse and his sons. Samuel goes in not knowing which of Jesse's sons would be the next king of Israel; he just knows one of them is the one that God has chosen. Samuel looks at these men through his natural carnal eyes. The same eyes that he looked through when Saul was selected; however, God was about to give Samuel a lesson on looking with the eyes of the spirit.

It is interesting to note that this was Samuel the prophet, not just anyone. This is the man that God honored every word that came from his lips. This shows us that even the most anointed among us can still give into the flesh at times, and this was one of those times.

This portion of the story should wake us all up to the reality that we can (and often do) make the mistake of establishing the wrong people to be our leaders and for the wrong reasons. Churches have suffered severely because the church leaders merely looked the part, but lacked the calling and anointing for the part. Nations have suffered because presidents and leaders were voted in simply because of some clever catch phrase, instead of an actual ability to lead the country to health and strength. It seems like the one that looks best in front of the camera gets the job. Is it not sad that we have settled for outside appearances over depth, character, and substance? Is it not sad that we have become so shallow?

1 Samuel 16:6-7)

> [6] So it was, when they came, that he looked at Eliab and said, "Surely the LORD's anointed is before Him!" But the LORD said to Samuel, "Do not look at his appearance or at his physical stature because I have refused him. For the LORD does not see as man sees; for man looks at the outward appearance, but the LORD looks at the heart."

Samuel looks at the eldest son of Jesse in the same manner as he looked at Saul, but God had rejected Eliab as king. God schools Samuel on how to find the right man for the position of king: *"Do not look at his appearance or at his physical stature… but the LORD looks at the heart."*

Again, we all should learn from this. All the ones that looked good in the suit and looked good behind the pulpit were rejected. Jesse brings seven of his sons to Samuel, and God rejects them all because each one fulfilled what man would want in a king. God was showing Samuel what He wanted in a king.

Found and Anointed as King

1 Samuel 16:11-12)

> *And Samuel said to Jesse, "Are all the young men here?" Then he said, "There remains yet the youngest, and there he is, keeping the sheep." And Samuel said to Jesse, "Send and bring him. For we will not sit down till he comes here."* ¹² *So he sent and brought him in. Now he was ruddy, with bright eyes, and good-looking. And the LORD said, "Arise, anoint him; for this is the one!"*

After Samuel had stood before each of the sons that Jesse presented, God rejected them all. Asking Jesse if any other sons were missed, Jesse points out that the youngest was out with the sheep. David, the youngest of Jesse's sons, was not even invited to the party. Jesse himself, David's father, did not even think David was important enough to be invited to the event that hosted Samuel. David was rejected by his father, but His heavenly Father had not rejected him.

Notice that David was close by, but still not part of the festivities. David was busy tending to the sheep. In other words, David was simply found doing what he was supposed to be doing. Once David stood before Samuel, the LORD said, *"Arise, anoint him; for this is the one!"* The one rejected by his father and yet still remained faithful, was the one that inherited the throne and the nation.

The seemingly insignificant one - not even invited to the party - was the one God chose as king over His people.

We MUST learn to look beyond outward appearances and look at the heart.

God often rejects what seems to be the best choice and will choose the underdog at times. As I have said many times before, God is raising up that which seems insignificant and small. It is these that will do great things in the earth. The David generation is in the field with the few sheep, being trained by God to lead his people. The Sauls of this generation are about to be replaced by the Davids that God is raising up. The question I have is, "Will we recognize these Davids as the leaders God has chosen when they come out of the fields?"

The Horn and the Flask

1 Samuel 16:.1

> Fill your horn with oil, and go; I am sending you to Jesse the Bethlehemite. For I have provided Myself a king among his sons."

It is interesting that God gives explicit instruction about the vessel that Samuel was to use in anointing David as the King of Israel. God tells Samuel to fill his horn with oil. This is different than the way Saul was anointed. Saul was anointed with oil from a flask (vial).

1 Samuel 10:1

> Then Samuel took a flask of oil and poured it on his head, and kissed him and said: "Is it not because the LORD has anointed you commander over His inheritance?

This may not seem like a big deal, but it is when you look at the life and leadership of Saul compared to the life and leadership of David, that you see why this is important. It is interesting to note that the anointing oil is the same, but the vessels that it comes from are different. Saul is anointed from a flask - a flask is man-made. David is anointed from a horn (most-likely a horn from an animal used as a sacrifice) – a horn is God-made.

Saul was made king because the people wanted a king just like the other nations. Although the anointing oil is the same, it came through the desires and work of man. David was a king after God's own heart. David was a king of God's making and desire. Often we establish and follow leaders that seem to be everything we want in a leader.

We tend to follow leaders that:

- Look the part.
- Sound the part.
- Have all the right catch phrases.
- Know the right people.
- Come from the right families.
- Are seemingly the most educated, etc.

This causes us to sometimes miss the ones that God has set up as His leader. Could you imagine if we learned to look at leadership in the same way God does?

What would the church look like if we learned to follow ONLY those that were anointed from the horn that God provides?

Not merely those that are anointed, but those that God says are of His heart? It is apparent that many have been anointed from the vessels of man and not the vessel of God. These Davids of our time will carry powerful anointings that come from the horn of God, not the flask of man. These will be the ones that lead

God's people from a heart that is after God's heart. These will be the people that seek after the glory of God instead of basking in their own glory.

Some have been rejected by man because they did not look like they had what it takes to lead God's people, but God has selected them for such a time as this. Others are those that have been diligently serving God by serving their 'fathers' even when their fathers have rejected them. They have been faithful in tending a few sheep; they have shown themselves faithful in what they have been entrusted with, which prepared them for more – much more!

We have been watching as many of our leaders have fallen into sin. We have watched as many of them have rejected the process of restoration that God would have them adhere to. As heartbreaking as this is, do not get discouraged or give up. A little David is being trained in the field with just a few sheep. These Davids are about to come crashing on the scene, and they will know how to bring freedom to God's people from the modern Philistines that have invaded our land. This is a time to be encouraged not discouraged!

Chapter 8
Kings in Training

The anointing and empowering of God did not leave Saul because he had sinned. The anointing and empowering to function as king left Saul when David was chosen and anointed by Samuel. This is something we need to keep in mind.

When the anointing leaves us,
it is not because we sinned,
but because someone else has taken our place.

Sometimes it is not because we sinned
that we lose the anointing, but because we
refused to overcome sin and get busy using
what God has given us.

This principle is seen in the stories of the talents and the minas.

Matthew 25:24

²⁴ *"Then he who had received the one talent came and said, 'Lord, I knew you to be a hard man, reaping where you have not sown, and gathering where you have not scattered seed.*

Matthew 25:28-29

²⁸ So take the talent from him, and give it to him who has ten talents.

²⁹ 'For to everyone who has, more will be given, and he will have abundance; but from him who does not have, even what he has will be taken away.

When we will not use what God has given us, or we do not use it correctly, we will lose it to someone that will use it as it is supposed to be used. The Spirit of the LORD left Saul because he refused to be obedient to the LORD by using the anointing and power in a manner that was consistent with the will of God for the position of a king. Saul used his position as king, and thus the anointing as king, for his purposes and pleasure. He did not use what God had given him to be obedient to the will of God but used it as he saw fit.

The stories of the talents and minas should be a wakeup call for every church leader. Join these stories with the story of Saul and we can clearly see that we MUST be busy doing exactly what God anointed and empowered us for.

Saul should have acted like a God-fearing king instead of a people-pleasing puppet. Church leaders should act like they actually love God with all their heart and being, and then lead from that place (we must actually love God with everything). When I say, "act," I am not talking about acting as if on a stage, but actually living it out in a real way. It must become part of who we are.

God Trains David to be King

1 Samuel 16:15-23

¹⁵ *And Saul's servants said to him, "Surely, a distressing spirit from God is troubling you.*

¹⁶ *Let our master now command your servants, who are before you, to seek out a man who is a skillful player on the harp. And it shall be that he will play it with his hand when the distressing spirit from God is upon you, and you shall be well."*

¹⁷ *So Saul said to his servants, "Provide me now a man who can play well, and bring him to me."*

¹⁸ *Then one of the servants answered and said, "Look, I have seen a son of Jesse the Bethlehemite, who is skillful in playing, a mighty man of valor, a man of war, prudent in speech, and a handsome person; and the LORD is with him."*

¹⁹ *Therefore Saul sent messengers to Jesse, and said, "Send me your son David, who is with the sheep."*

²⁰ *And Jesse took a donkey loaded with bread, a skin of wine, and a young goat, and sent them by his son David to Saul.*

²¹ *So David came to Saul and stood before him. And he loved him greatly, and he became his armor-bearer.*

²² *Then Saul sent to Jesse, saying, "Please let David stand before me, for he has found favor in my sight."*

²³ *And so it was, whenever the spirit from God was upon Saul, that David would take a harp and play it with his hand. Then Saul would become refreshed and well, and the distressing spirit would depart from him.*

God has a strange way of preparing us for the call that He has for us. David was the anointed king, but the extent of his training was a shepherd of the sheep. God provided a means for David to be close to the king in the king's palace so that he could know how to make the transition from shepherd to king. David learned a great deal about leadership from leading sheep in the field, but now he needed to know how to properly lead people from the throne.

God asks us this question, *"who has despised the day of small things?" (Zechariah 4:10).* This question is posed in a way as to get us to think and ponder the greater truth it highlights. The answer I believe is, "the fool despises the day of small things." We are to learn from everything in our life, including those times that it seems as if nothing of value is happening.

Several years ago I worked in a secular job that I absolutely hated. I knew I was called into the ministry and always felt as if this job was beneath me and standing in my way of my true calling. Every day was torture as I left for work because I was sure I was created for greater things. I was employed in this job for 12 years and each year felt like a decade. I never appreciated this job or my position as I should have.

In a strange way, I was eventually able to go into full-time ministry and plant a church. I never had to go back to outside work for over 15 years. I never had to physically go back, but emotionally and spiritually I had to return. I had to go back to my previous bosses and repent for my bad attitude and poor work ethic while employed with them. Why? Because God dealt with me and showed me that this secular job was my training ground. God put me in place to teach me how to work with and relate to the types of people I was to minister to. I could have turned my 12-year stay into a three-year stay if my attitude had been better. If I had only gleaned what I needed to learn, God would not have had to keep me in that job so long. I could have been in the fullness of my calling much sooner.

Looking back at this secular job and the work I did, I now realize that it was a great job and I had the opportunity to do great ministry in that place. I did my best to be a good example of what a Christian was supposed to be (for the most part), but had my heart and head been in the game I would have made a much greater impact much quicker than I did. There should have been more fuit for my labors had my heart been right.

My story, unfortunately, is not an isolated one. Many have gone through similar struggles while trying to work into the position they know deep down they were created for; instead of working from the anointing and position they were already in. The truth be told, if my heart were right, I would have been content with the 'pulpit' that God had given me amongst the people I was working with for 40 hours each week. God gave me a congregation to lead and minister to, but all I could see was that I was not in a church among people that said "amen" to everything I said. My heart was not right, so it took me 12 years to make a three-year impact. For me, the transition was made only after I learned what I needed to learn, and what took me 12 years to learn I should have learned in three. Oh, did I mention that it took me 12 years to make a three-year impact?

Always remember,
we were designed to be full of the Spirit.
We will never be truly empty at any time.

We will either be full of the Spirit of the LORD,
or we will be full of some other spirit.

Saul found this out the hard way. When we take what God has given us and faithfully use it we will be full of the anointing and Holy Spirit of the LORD, fully empowered for our calling. When the Spirit of God was taken from Saul and given to David, Saul received a "distressing spirit from God." This distressing spirit drove Saul mad and caused him to need something to bring relief from the distress he was experiencing. This is where David comes in.

1 Samuel 16:16-20

> ¹⁶ *Let our master now command your servants, who are before you, to seek out a man who is a skillful player on the harp. And it shall be that he will play it with his hand when the distressing spirit from God is upon you, and you shall be well."*
>
> ¹⁷ *So Saul said to his servants, "Provide me now a man who can play well, and bring him to me."*
>
> ¹⁸ *Then one of the servants answered and said, "Look, I have seen a son of Jesse the Bethlehemite, who is skillful in playing, a mighty man of valor, a man of war, prudent in speech, and a handsome person; and the LORD is with him."*
>
> ¹⁹ *Therefore Saul sent messengers to Jesse, and said, "Send me your son David, who is with the sheep."*
>
> ²⁰ *And Jesse took a donkey loaded with bread, a skin of wine, and a young goat, and sent them by his son David to Saul.*

Instead of the Spirit of the LORD, Saul was given a distressing spirit instead. If we are disobedient and refuse to use righteously what God has provided us with, then we will lose what we were entrusted with. When this distressing spirit would come upon Saul the only relief was found when David would play his instrument. The anointing and power of God would flow

116

through the music that David played for the troubled king. Not only did this bring relief to Saul but it made way for David to come into the palace. When Saul received this distressing spirit, it opened the way for David to obtain the training he needed to rule as king. David was now in the palace at Saul's right hand because of a distressing spirit.

Many people today have a warped view of God's love. Many would read this and try to explain how God would never send a distressing spirit to anyone, as they point out that a God of love would never do such a thing. We MUST stop using the world's definition of love when speaking of God and the things of God. We MUST understand that God did send a distressing spirit to someone because the Bible says He did. We must realize that God will do what He must do to lead us where He wants us to be. Sending Saul a distressing spirit led to David being trained as king, and resulted in David ruling with a heart after God.

The story of Saul and the distressing spirit is not an Old Testament truth and principle only.

The idea of God sending someone a distressing spirit is found in the New Testament as well.

This is what Paul did to a brother that refused to repent of his sin.

1 Corinthians 5:4-5

> *⁴ In the name of our Lord Jesus Christ, when you are gathered together, along with my spirit, with the power of our Lord Jesus Christ,*
>
> *⁵ deliver such a one to Satan for the destruction of the flesh that his spirit may be saved on the day of the Lord Jesus.*

117

1 Timothy 1:20

> ...*of whom are Hymenaeus and Alexander, whom I delivered to Satan that they may learn not to blaspheme.*

This is harsh, but loving. In both cases, the people in question were in danger of losing their salvation or may not have actually been saved at all. In both instances, until they repented they were in a very real risk of going to hell. In v.5 of 1 Corinthians 5, we see why this is a loving thing to do at times: *"that his spirit may be saved on the day of the Lord Jesus."* This is the last resort to get people saved. Often hardship causes people to see how much they need the Lord. God NEVER would send a distressing spirit to someone unless it was the last resort, after all other options run out.

Saul could now clearly see that he needed to be restored in his relationship with God. Saul could now understand the distinction between himself and David. It was still his choice to repent and seek God or continue going the way he was going, but he now understood that he needed to make a change.

This is one of the reasons why I am so BIG on praise and worship. An anointed psalmist can bring great spiritual freedom and release to all those around him/her. At my church, we do not put a time limit on praise and worship. We worship the LORD over an hour every Sunday morning and often up to two hours. We do this because this is the portion of the service that is ALL about God. The sermon is for the people, but the praise and worship are for the LORD. I would rather give God the greater portion of our time, energy and adoration than what we would give to one another.

In my life and ministry, I have seen more people healed and delivered in praise and worship than in a prayer line. When God is pleased with our *"sacrifice of praise" (Hebrews 13:15)*, He shows His pleasure by setting us free from what binds us. When God is present, everything of Satan's must bow and leave. We must learn to give ourselves completely in praise and worship, and as we do this, we can receive more fully from the presence of the LORD.

1 Samuel 16:18

Then one of the servants answered and said, "Look, I have seen a son of Jesse the Bethlehemite, who is skillful in playing, a mighty man of valor, a man of war, prudent in speech, and a handsome person; and the LORD is with him."

It is interesting to note that David had not yet been in a battle, nor had he ever had a position that these things could be recognized. Remember, he was not viewed as important enough to be invited to the party by his father. These servants of Saul were actually prophesying about David.

It is also interesting to note that Saul could prophesy only when he was around the prophets. Saul's servants seemed to be able to prophesy when they were around Saul. More indication that Saul was not using what he was entrusted with, but his servants were. It seems as if Saul's servant learned how to operate in the prophetic anointing that was entrusted to Saul. It is wonderful that someone was willing to use this gift, but how much more powerful would it have been if Saul had used what was entrusted to him, instead of his servants? Keep this in mind,

"You may lose what you do not use."
Use everything that God has given you for His
glory.

Saul Loves David

1 Samuel 16:21-23

> [21] *So David came to Saul and stood before him. And he loved him greatly, and he became his armor-bearer.*
>
> [22] *Then Saul sent to Jesse, saying, "Please let David stand before me, for he has found favor in my sight."*
>
> [23] *And so it was, whenever the spirit from God was upon Saul, that David would take a harp and play it with his hand. Then Saul would become refreshed and well, and the distressing spirit would depart from him.*

David is summoned by King Saul to play his instrument and drive away the distressing spirit he was given. The music David played brought great relief to Saul when he was being assaulted by the spirit that distressed him. Saul comes to love David significantly and makes David his armor bearer. This fact shows at this point Saul trusted David with his life. Saul knew that David had to keep watch over him in battle. David would be the closest person to the king with a weapon in his hand. For a king to bring someone that close to himself and put a weapon in his hand was to say, "I trust you with my life."

At this point in the story, Saul and David had a great and healthy relationship with one another. This is the type of relationship that God would want his leaders to have today. Church leaders should be close enough together that we cover one another, guard one another, and trust one another with our lives. It is unfortunate, but these types of relationships are rare – very rare! This needs to change.

Saul asks Jesse to allow David to remain in the palace with him. Saul not only loved David as a servant but as a son. This put David in a position to learn a great deal about how to be king. Not only would David see what to do, but also what not to do as king. David could now see firsthand what works and what does not work as a king.

In this regard, Saul was right in bringing David under his wing to raise him up in the palace. Saul never realized that he was training his replacement, but he was right in bringing in the one that was anointed to help him become a better king. At this point, Saul was doing the right thing for the right reasons, and we can learn from this. We should do the same types of things.

When people of quality and character are anointed in an area we are weak in, we should bring them in to help us in our area of weakness. In the case of Saul, David was needed to drive away a distressing spirit. This might not be your weak point, but each of us has weaknesses that we could use an anointed David to help in our areas of weakness, but for us to do this, we must first be able to admit that we need help. Humility of heart is needed by any leader; the humility that leads to the understanding of weakness, then the filling of that position with someone that is stronger in that given area.

The Armor Bearer Syndrome

I want to address the 'armor bearer' syndrome in the modern church today. To be blunt, this idea has been exploited and misused to the point of absurdity and often downright foolishness. This needs to be addressed because many are being used as nothing more than slaves for misguided leaders, all under the title of 'armor bearer'.

Armor bearers (Biblically speaking), were the warriors that accompanied the king or other soldiers in battle. They were warriors themselves that had the responsibility to fight alongside another warrior, carrying extra armor and weapons of the warrior he was assigned to. As the armor bearers, they would also finish the job the soldier left behind.

Imagine that a warrior with sword in hand was hacking his way through the battlefield. He would not have time to make sure everyone that he struck with his sword was dead or completely incapacitated, so his armor bearer would come behind him and finish the job. So as the warrior is fighting and making his way through the enemy lines, the armor bearer would follow behind him and make sure that the enemy was actually dead, as he kept an eye on the weapons and armor of the warrior.

Does that sound like a modern-day armor bearer? Of course not! The position of armor bearer was only relevant on the battlefield. What is pictured above looks nothing like the current armor bearer that many church leaders have around them.

Today's armor bearer looks more like a butler (and sometimes slave) than a warrior in battle. Today's armor bearers are chauffeurs, personal assistants, and servants, not real armor bearers. It is sad but we can find books and seminars geared at training people to be armor bearers, and in the end, no one walks away with armor or a sword.

This is not only wrong, but false in its ideology and the theology behind it. This has to be made right in the church today. I personally know pastors that expect others to carry their Bible and sermon outline to the pulpit. They also expect others to serve them their food at the fellowships, and to get them their drink. I know some that expect others to pick up their dry cleaning, wash their car, and take care of all their needs. This is a disgusting abuse of people's time, energy, and faithfulness.

Please do not misunderstand me: some have a real gift of helps that thrive when they help others, especially those in leadership. These persons should be employed to help in some of these areas, but it should NEVER be demanded! Once it is demanded, it becomes witchcraft due to the manipulation that goes with it. A person that has a real gift of helps will do these things from a pure heart to help and not because he or she was manipulated into it.

The control I have witnessed pastors using over people all in the name of 'armor bearer' has been disgusting. I have seen marriages strained to the point of breaking, all because a pastor demands his armor bearer to be at his beck and call at all times. Usually, that call comes while at the dinner table or when he should have been at his kid's game. If the armor bearer does not jump the moment the pastor calls, then he is blasted from the pulpit the following Sunday for being rebellious. Sound familiar?

This has got to stop! This type of abuse is rampant in the church world today. When this kind of abuse is present in a church, it closes the door to a genuine gift of helps and replaces it with a culturally developed office of an armor bearer. By the way, NO SUCH OFFICE EXISTS! The position of armor bearer was never an office to be filled. It was a position occupied by a warrior, for a warrior, and for the battlefield. Not a church leader for a church member to make the pastor look and feel important.

Many reading this have a call of God upon them and their life but have yet to fully step into the position they know they are anointed for. You may be asking, "Why?" and "How long?" Many of you are like David, serving in the house of Saul. Be encouraged! You are being trained by the Sauls of today – the very ones you will be replacing.

Some of you are frustrated because you know you have more than the people you are working for. You know that you are the one that drives out the darkness and replaces it with light. You may be responsible for the peace of God that fills your church because you are driving out the distressing spirits that have been plaguing the church leadership. Keep doing what you are called and anointed to do in this season. Remember, David carried the anointing to rule as king, but was found driving away a distressing spirit from the fallen king he was to replace. David remained faithful to Saul and to the position he was entrusted with at the time. This you must do as well.

You must stay true to the position
you have been placed in until God removes you.

You are being trained for something much bigger.

Chapter 9
Becoming Stewards

Just as Israel experienced powerful transitions from Eli to Samuel and Saul to David, we are witnessing similar changes in the church today. God is removing those who have a mere "form of godliness" and replacing them with those who are in pursuit of Him (1 Timothy 3:5). God is no longer tolerating those who are committed in form only and is removing those who are His only in name. We are in the days when calling oneself a Christian is not enough. God is looking for those who live as faithful followers of Jesus. Our words and titles will not suffice in the days ahead because our religious titles will not be enough.

Quoting Isaiah 29:13, Jesus spoke these words:

Matthew 15:8

> *These people draw near to Me with their mouth and honor Me with their lips, but their heart is far from Me.*

Throughout history God dealt with His people when they fell into serving Him in word only. God is dealing with His people today in a similar manner. Just as judgment begins "at the house of God" (1 Peter 4:17), this judgment is starting with those who are the stewards of the house of God. The ones that are supposed to establish and steward the "widespread revelation" (1 Samuel 3:1) of our day are being scrutinized by Heaven as we speak. Those who have had a passion to know God intimately will excel in the next season of our history, but those who have known Christ in name only will be removed and replaced by those who are seemingly inexperienced but have a harp in their hand and smell like the sheep that Jesus loves.

Here are some things that we are witnessing in our day and age:

- Just as the Spirit of God left Saul when Samuel anointed David, we will see this happen over and over in our day and age.
- Just as Saul surrounded himself with people that were more in tune with God while he had lost his personal relationship with God, we will see present day leaders attempt to preserve their ministries in a similar manner.
- Just as David received the Spirit that was taken from Saul, we have many Davids still in the fields that are about to receive the anointing of those that are falling, and...
- As David was trained to be king in the palace as he worked for Saul, many are presently being trained in the houses and churches that they will soon be leading.

God is setting us up for a great move of His Spirit. We are being prepared to steward what He gives us. Just as a steward of finance needs to know how to handle finances, we are being trained as stewards of God's house and kingdom. We are about to be given access to the Kingdom of Heaven as never before. Once this happens, we will be expected to steward what we have been given. A steward is one that manages what belongs to another (especially land and property). Our stewardship is about to extend into the Kingdom of God deeper and further than we have ever experienced.

This is the reason why these significant transitions are upon us. The Elis in the body of Christ are being removed so the Samuels can rise up and take their place. These Samuels will restore the word of the Lord that brings the breakthroughs needed to get the people of God positioned for the move of the Spirit we have been promised and are waiting for.

In a similar manner, the Sauls are being replaced by the Davids. God wants the kings and priests to arise in this hour. Samuel represents the anointing and power of God (priests), while David represents the authority to rule and reign as kings unto our God (Revelation 1:6; 5:10). When both of these are in place, a mighty move of the Spirit will sweep through the earth bringing millions (perhaps billions) to the Lord. It is unfortunate, but the present religious order simply does not have what it takes to steward a move of God as I just described. God will be removing many of the current kings and priests of today just because they refuse to become what they need to become for this next move of the Spirit. Simply put, they are stuck.

People that have positions of authority and prestige must realize that simply because of the position they hold, others will look to them and even want to be like them.

In other words, merely because of the title and position, these ones will set the standard for others around them. If we as leaders are stuck in yesterday's move, we will inevitably cause those around us to miss what God is presently doing. It is our job to remain on 'the cutting edge' of the Spirit, knowing what God is doing in the earth today and work to help establish a fresh and continual outpouring with those we have been entrusted with. This, of course, was true for Saul, and since he was king others would follow his lead. We find this concept at work in the story of Goliath.

1 Samuel 17:1-4

¹ Now the Philistines gathered their armies together to battle, and were gathered at Sochoh, which belongs to Judah; they encamped between Sochoh and Azekah, in Ephes Dammim.

² And Saul and the men of Israel were gathered together, and they encamped in the Valley of Elah and drew up in battle array against the Philistines.

³ The Philistines stood on a mountain on one side, and Israel stood on a mountain on the other side, with a valley between them.

⁴ And a champion went out from the camp of the Philistines, named Goliath, from Gath, whose height was six cubits and a span.

Goliath was the "champion" of the Philistines. The Philistines came to make war against Israel, so Saul and his army came and prepared themselves for war.

1 Samuel 17:8-11

⁸ Then he stood and cried out to the armies of Israel, and said to them, "Why have you come out to line up for battle? Am I not a Philistine, and you the servants of Saul? Choose a man for yourselves, and let him come down to me.

⁹ If he is able to fight with me and kill me, then we will be your servants. But if I prevail against him and kill him, then you shall be our servants and serve us."

¹⁰ And the Philistine said, "I defy the armies of Israel this day; give me a man, that we may fight together."

¹¹ When Saul and all Israel heard these words of the Philistine, they were dismayed and greatly afraid.

Just as we have been looking at the story of Saul and David and seeing that its truths apply to us today, this story is no different. The enemies of today have arrayed themselves for battle, and have set themselves on the hill overlooking the valley of our present day and culture. This enemy has been taunting God's people, even sending out their champions to mock and challenge the church and what it stands for. These champions of the enemy are such things as abortion, homosexuality, and humanism and those that support them. These champions of the modern Philistines have been taunting the church of today, and our Sauls are hiding in their tents, hoping for Jesus to return and save them. Since many of our rulers and leaders are acting as Saul did, the entire church today is being affected by the fear and dismay of the Sauls of today.

It is unfortunate that many church leaders have embraced the eschatological view that Jesus is about to come and get us any minute now to save us from a corrupt system that we have no control over.

The modern Goliath of this present darkness we are living in and the fear of antichrist have crippled many of our leaders today. Throw in the hype of the Blood Moons, the Shemitah, the

129

One World Government and the like, and it is plain to see who our modern Sauls are. They are the ones that are telling people to prepare for our departure instead of preparing the people to engage the culture, rid it of the modern Philistines, and bring godly change to the society around us. Saul hid in his church (tent) instead of leading his men in battle. It is time for a revolution!

The modern 'end-time' teaching has done more to hurt the church than help it.
Many saints are ready to check out and go home to glory instead of rolling up their sleeves to get busy changing society for the better.

I have challenged many in this area over the years, often being labeled a heretic, false teacher, false prophet, etc. Considering all that I have faced and all that I know of the end-time doctrine, I understand most all of it to be false.

Most of our end-time theology comes from fear and it births fear.
By this alone we should know that it is false doctrine.

Paul wrote this to Timothy:

2 Timothy 1:7

For God has not given us a spirit of fear, but of power and of love and of a sound mind.

Anything that produces fear in God's people is born of a false spirit.

130

The only fear we are allowed to harbor is "the fear of the Lord." What I have witnessed in those that are proponents of the end-time theology as it is taught in most churches is far from the fear of the Lord. Instead, it is fear of missing the rapture, fear of anti-Christ, fear of plagues and war, etc. None of these are to be in the heart of the believer, but this doctrine is freely taught by most preachers and without thought or care what it is doing to the listeners. When gone unchallenged, the people live in fear without any hope of a future. This type of mental and spiritual destruction must stop.

God, the God of the Bible said this:

Jeremiah 29:11

> *For I know the thoughts that I think toward you, says the LORD, thoughts of peace and not of evil, to give you a future and a hope.*

These are the words of the God I serve. As long as we have breath in our lungs, we have hope for a better tomorrow. God is all about hope and restoration, but the current end-time theology teachers have forgotten that and robbed people of the hope of a brighter future.

Part of the transition we are in
is the stripping away of all doctrines that have
been birthed in, and that produce fear,
or any other wicked mindset.

When we talk about modern day Sauls and Davids, we are speaking more of a state of heart and the actions that flow from that particular heart condition.

It is not one's age or era that determines
whether he or she is a Saul or a David;
instead, it is what one does consistently,
and consecutively that shows where they are.

It truly is a state of heart and the actions that flow from the heart that makes one a Saul or a David.

Matthew 12:35

A good man out of the good treasure of his heart brings forth good things, and an evil man out of the evil treasure brings forth evil things.

Proverbs 4:23

Keep your heart with all diligence, for out of it spring the issues of life.

This shows that no matter what state a church leader is in at this moment, they can repent and become what they need to become to steward the things God has for this generation. If they are open and honest about who they truly are, a grace is available to them that will cause them to embrace the David-like mindset and the anointing to accompany that way of thinking. Everything needed to overcome the Saul mindset is right now being offered to our leaders, but they will have to be completely open to changing themselves by allowing the presence of God and His anointing to completely rework, reestablish, and renew them in every way.

Saul had many chances presented to him by which he could have acted and reacted differently. He refused to change himself and the way he led the nation, so God made a way to have him replaced. It was not because Saul made one mistake, but because of years of rebellion toward God and God's will for him. Saul consistently put his desires and his fear of the people over the desires of God. At any time Saul could have done things differently, but he rebelled against the subtle promptings of the Spirit as well as the direct confrontations of the prophet. Saul continued doing what he desired, and in the end, God replaced him with David.

During this time in Israel's history, as well as in our present world, God is looking for champions of His own. God is looking for men and women that will stand up against the champions of the modern Philistines and bring them down. It is unfortunate, but we have too many Sauls that are more interested in self-preservation than facing off with the enemy.

What is interesting is that the word 'Philistine', in its biblical use, means 'immigrant'. An immigrant is someone that moves into an area that is not their own, and they do this usually uninvited. Immigrants will often come into an area and remain unless someone forces them out.

The word 'Philistine', as used in a modern sense, has come to mean 'someone that that is hostile to the culture around them'. A modern Philistine would be someone that comes into an area and demands that the people and culture of that area change to their liking, instead of assimilating into the culture of the area they are now in.

The Philistines are not only a group of people we read about in the pages of scripture, but are very much alive and active today. Modern Philistines have invaded our land and are hostile to everything we hold dear. The Philistines of today are found in the homosexual (LGBT) movement, the Islamic invasion of the west, the political correctness movement, and political and ideological movements such as liberalism and socialism. These Philistines have moved in uninvited by the populace and have been hostile towards the Christian values that have kept our nation strong for many years. These Philistines have their champions shouting their propaganda and swaying people into their false philosophies, while our Sauls are hiding away in their tents, afraid of facing these giants, as well as the people and ideologies they represent.

What is needed today are the Davids that are unafraid of the Philistines and their champions. Davids that will face these demonic ideologies and remove their heads, rendering them powerless.

We need a company of Davids that will not hide
in the church and spout weak-kneed religious
messages of tolerance and coexistence,
but a company of warriors that are able to
articulate and fight on the battlefield of ideas.

Remember, the Philistines were on one side of the valley, and the army of Israel was on the other side of the valley. For 40 consecutive days, morning and evening, Goliath the Philistine champion would come out to defy the armies of Israel. This caused "Saul and all Israel" to become filled with fear and hide from the enemy.

1 Samuel 17:11

When Saul and all Israel heard these words of the Philistine,
they were dismayed and greatly afraid.

This is a great story of 'follow the leader'. The army of Israel became terrified every time Goliath came to the battlefield, not necessarily because of Goliath himself, but because Saul their king and commander was terrified. Those who were under Saul's leadership merely responded as they saw their king respond (v.11, *"Saul and all Israel heard these words of the Philistine, they were dismayed and greatly afraid"*). Saul was supposed to be the one that stood up against the enemies of his people and his kingdom. When he showed that he was afraid of this Philistine champion, everyone under his care became afraid as well.

Church leaders must understand this concept.

The people under our care will take upon themselves the attitudes and characteristics we display.

The people became afraid of the Philistines and their champion because the leader of Israel was afraid. The people simply did what they were supposed to do; they followed Saul, but Saul did not lead as he was supposed to. On account of Saul's failure to lead as he was supposed to, the people were led into a self-destructive mindset that could have literally cost them their lives. Had they remained in their fear, the nation could have been lost to the Philistines.

A New Leader Arises

1 Samuel 17:32

> *Then David said to Saul, "Let no man's heart fail because of him; your servant will go and fight with this Philistine."*

When David came to the battlefield and heard the taunts of Goliath and saw that no one from the camp of Israel would go out to meet him in battle, David volunteered to fight the giant. At this point, David was still viewed as a mere youth, too young to be in the army and too young for battle, but he was the only one brave enough to face the giant. Call it bravery or stupidity, either way, David was the only one willing to face the giant that taunted God's people.

This is often played out in our modern age. Those that are supposed to be facing the giants of the day hide away in their tents (offices or churches), not willing to enter the battle and face the giants of the day. Those that are coming onto the scene are facing the issues and problems (giants) that have been taunting the church and stopping us from being productive. These Davids are leading the charge onto the battlefield often entirely by themselves because the Sauls and their armies are hiding on account of their fear.

When you read this story, it is plain to see just how crippling fear is. Fear of the enemy (those that taunt the church) often keep us hiding away from the enemy and the battle we are supposed to be engaged in. It is interesting to take note of all the believers that are active members of a church but not active 'Christian' members of society. Far too many of us know how to be good Christians on Sunday, but have yet to know how to be good citizens on Monday. We have not learned how to go out of the church building with the same fervency and anointing as we enjoyed while in it. Far too many have yet to learn how to take the power and anointing from the church and manifest it in the marketplace and the culture around them.

God is raising up a company of Davids
that will blaze the trail and lead the way
to the battlefield.

Goliath Loses His Head

1 Samuel 17:48-51

[48] *So it was when the Philistine arose and came and drew near to meet David, that David hurried and ran toward the army to meet the Philistine.*

[49] *Then David put his hand in his bag and took out a stone, and he slung it and struck the Philistine in his forehead so that the stone sank into his forehead, and he fell on his face to the earth.*

[50] *So David prevailed over the Philistine with a sling and stone, and struck the Philistine and killed him. But there was no sword in the hand of David.*

[51] *Therefore David ran and stood over the Philistine, took his sword and drew it out of its sheath and killed him, and cut off his head with it. And when the Philistines saw that their champion was dead, they fled.*

Think about this – David was not deemed important enough to be invited to the party when Samuel came looking for the new king to rule over God's people. David was ridiculed by his brother for being young and a mere shepherd boy. King Saul did not think David was old enough or experienced enough to face Goliath, and yet it was David that took Goliath's head. This is what we are going to be seeing more and more.

Those that are stuck in the previous move of God are the greatest critics of the leaders of the new move of God.

Keep this in mind:

Just because some are fearless does not automatically make them foolish.

However, God can still use the foolish and their foolishness for His purpose.

1 Samuel 17:52-54

> [52] *Now the men of Israel and Judah arose and shouted, and pursued the Philistines as far as the entrance of the valley and to the gates of Ekron. And the wounded of the Philistines fell along the road to Shaaraim, even as far as Gath and Ekron.*

> [53] *Then the children of Israel returned from chasing the Philistines, and they plundered their tents.*

> [54] *And David took the head of the Philistine and brought it to Jerusalem, but he put his armor in his tent.*

David had the courage and showed lots of faith in God as well as the strength of character and heart. David never wavered at any point. David never backed down from his enemy. It is recorded that, "David hurried and ran toward the army to meet the Philistine." David ran to the battle, not away from it! David not only brought down the giant, but he brought courage to the entire army of Israel.

This foolish little boy not only brought down the giant, but imparted to the army of Israel courage and strength after he took

Goliath's head. The men of Israel, now filled with courage, pursued and struck down the fleeing Philistines. Just moments before, they were filled with fear and dismay.

Once the catalyst of fear is brought down,
strength and courage can return.

Goliath can represent a principality or a stronghold in a region. When an ungodly stronghold of a spirit is over a region, the people become subject to whatever that stronghold may be. In this case, it was fear and discouragement because of Goliath. It may not be the same type of fear and despair, but the principle is the same.

Whatever the principality is over a region,
the people of that region will take upon them
the characteristics of that principality.

Once these features are embraced and given into, a stronghold develops. Once a stronghold is established, it is difficult to break its power because nearly everyone is in agreement with its existence, even if they do not realize it.

When those who are supposed to bring down
the stronghold of the enemy give into and agree
with the stronghold, it will take one that is like
David to bring the stronghold down that
has captured everyone else.

It is unfortunate that in the modern day church leadership we have not had an abundance of giant killers. If we are honest, we will all agree that this is true. This nation and the world have been embracing such things as the homosexual agenda, the

Muslim invasion of the West, abortion-on-demand, human trafficking, the sex trade, etc. Why is this happening? Simply because we have had a generation of Elis and Sauls leading the church.

> *When we have weak and compromising*
> *leadership in the church, it always leads*
> *to weak and compromising leadership*
> *outside of the church.*

When I say weak and compromising leadership in the church, I am not talking about the inability to keep the local church afloat, or to maintain the ministries of the church. I am speaking about church leadership that refuses to address the issues that plague the society and culture around them. These are the church leaders that are too cowardly to speak out against adultery, homosexuality, abortion, political correctness, pornography, etc. These are the church leaders that refuse to talk about eternal damnation for those that deny Jesus. These are the ones that have relegated themselves to official 'ear-tickler' status.

Please do not misunderstand me. I am not suggesting that ALL pastors and preachers fall into the category of "weak and compromising." However, it seems that for every one that is willing to speak on these subjects openly and with conviction, ten others are watering down the truth, stroking egos and tickling ears. It is time for a revolution! We must return to speaking on these things and bring down the strongholds that have been holding our culture and society in a stupor.

Ephesians 6:12

> For we do not wrestle against flesh and blood, but against
> principalities, against powers, against the rulers of the darkness
> of this age, against spiritual hosts of wickedness in the heavenly
> places.

When Goliath was brought down, all the Philistines ran and scattered. Regarding the Israelites, fear changed to courage and the Israelites ended up plundering the tents of the enemy. This is what happens when the Davids of our age rise up and bring down the giants before us: the enemy will scatter. This is the picture of real regional spiritual warfare.

> **When we bring down the principality
> over the region, all the lesser spirits lose
> their authority and power to remain.**

At that point, we can plunder and take what the enemy has held onto.

> **We need leaders that are no longer comfortable
> merely behind the pulpits of their church, but are
> equally comfortable behind the podiums of
> societal transformation.**

When these leaders rise up, you will see the Goliaths of our day and age come crashing down while losing their heads. Whose characteristics will you take upon yourself? The characteristics of Eli who did not want to 'rock the boat' and left his sons to continue in sin? Or maybe the characteristics of Samuel? He restored the true word of the Lord and brought the nation back to God. Perhaps you will be more like Saul? Begin strong but finish in humiliation because the will of the people is more important than the will of God. Then again, you can be like David, a man after God's own heart. David, who was willing to face the giant of the day and take off its head.

We need leaders in the church that will rise up with the word in their mouth like Samuel, and a sword in their hand like David. The choice is ours to make. The choice is yours to make. Whose characteristics will you embrace?

Chapter 10
The Challenge of Obscurity

We found that under the leadership of Saul all of Israel, including the army, was full of fear on account of Goliath and his taunts. The people became afraid because their leader (Saul) was scared. This shows us that...

> *People will follow a leader even when*
> *that leader is failing to lead as he should.*

Saul was not a failure as a leader because he actually led the people. What caused him to be a failure was *how* he led the people, and *what* he led them into. This shows us that Saul had everything needed to become a great king because of his leadership skills. It is sad that he led the people into the wrong things. Here in the story of Goliath, Saul led the people into fear and dismay. He was the king and influential leader that could have led his people into courage and victory.

David (as a young man) comes and does what Saul should have done. David went to battle and killed Goliath. Goliath was the giant champion of the Philistines that was responsible for causing fear to grip Saul and his army. At this point, most believe that David was about 16 or 17 years of age. Here a teenager is doing what the king and commander of God's people would not do. This simple fact that David was willing to face the giant should have been enough to prompt Saul to face Goliath on the battlefield, but instead, he sent David to do his job.

Before David, we find no 'giant killers' in Israel. Instead, the army and nation were afraid of just one giant because Saul was afraid of that one giant. This is interesting and sad at the same time, but this is happening all around us today. Many are in fear of things just because a leader is in fear of it. As I pointed out with the end-time theology that is being preached today, many are in fear of the future because of the way this doctrine is being pushed on the church today. Many leaders are pushing this doctrine as if it were on the same level as the doctrine of salvation. It is sad that many are cowering in fear because of this teaching, and teachings like it. Fearful preachers are pushing their fear onto the body of Christ, and many are giving into it.

Many giants have come against the church today. Some of these giants have been embraced and propped up from the pulpit. I am speaking of the giants of defeatist end-time theology; 'greasy grace (hyper-grace)' ideologies that remove individual responsibility; fundamentalist teachings that say the gifts and power of the Holy Spirit are no longer in the church, etc. These are giants in the church, and where these types of ideologies are being espoused, the people are becoming what these ideologies are declaring – fearful, irresponsible, and weak.

It is time for a revolution of glory and power in the church, but it will not happen until we have a revolution in what is taught from the pulpits.

After David rose up as a giant killer, at least four other giant killers came up after him.

Remember,
you become what you are under.

Whatever your covering is,
you will become as well.

This is a principle that must be understood. I know people that have almost nothing good to say about the church they attend. Once, while in a conversation with someone that complained a great deal about the church they attended, I asked, "Then why do you go?" Their answer was, "Well they have a good children's ministry." So this family attended a church they did not like or appreciate only because of the children's ministry, all the while becoming the very thing they were complaining about. That is simply how it works. Each of us will receive an impartation from the leadership of the church we attend, making us into that which is over us. We all need to meditate upon and answer this question: "What are you under?" Because that is what you are becoming.

Someone that has the heart of David would find a church that was Spirit-filled and on fire; then join, get involved and create a great children's ministry (or whatever was needed). Giant killers do just that, they kill giants. They do not get lost in a church that they will not grow in just because it has one thing going for it. They will get involved in a church that has the potential to increase into a training ground for giant killers.

If your church is not being led by a giant killer
and already producing giant killers,
then it most likely never will.

If your church is being led by a giant killer
and has produced even one giant killer,
then it can grow and produce much more.

Always remember,
you become what you are under.
Under Saul everyone was afraid,
but under David everyone had courage.
What are you under?

Coming out of Obscurity

1 Samuel 17:12-15

> [12] *Now David was the son of that Ephrathite of Bethlehem Judah, whose name was Jesse, and who had eight sons. And the man was old, advanced in years, in the days of Saul.*

> [13] *The three oldest sons of Jesse had gone to follow Saul to the battle. The names of his three sons who went to the battle were Eliab the firstborn, next to him Abinadab, and the third Shammah.*

> [14] *David was the youngest. And the three oldest followed Saul.*

> [15] *But David occasionally went and returned from Saul to feed his father's sheep at Bethlehem.*

David's brothers (Eliab, Abinadab, and Shammah) joined Saul in the battle against the Philistines. All three of them heard the taunts of Goliath for 40 days straight. David at this point was also employed by Saul as the king's personal deliverance minister. David would play for the king whenever the distressing spirit from God would come upon him. As David played, the spirit would retreat, bringing temporary relief to Saul. At least four sons of Jesse were employed as soldiers by Saul; three in his natural army and one in the supernatural army.

David would return to his home and father to help with the flocks. David spent most of his time with Saul in the palace, but he would often return home to help his father with the sheep. Even though David had a lofty position working for the king in the palace, he still had the heart for his father and the sheep he would tend. This is important to understand the heart and character of David. He did not forget where he came from because he often went back and helped on the family farm. This is the quality of leadership God wants to see arise today.

Often we see people build a name for themselves, then forget who they really are and where they have come from. God wants leaders that will remain humble enough to roll up their sleeves and milk the cow. Until we have leaders that remain humble as David did, we will not have a sustained move of God in the earth.

We are introduced to Saul in the story of his father's donkeys that go missing (1 Samuel 9). Saul went looking for the donkeys and could not find them. Contrast this story with David in 1 Samuel 17, and you will conclude that David was far more diligent regarding his duties as a son and as a shepherd. While Saul was looking for his father's donkeys that had escaped, David is found taking constant care of his father's sheep. Saul wanted to quit looking for the lost donkeys after three days, while David fought lions and bears while protecting the sheep, and held down another job working for the king as well. This is just one of the reasons we find that David was a man after God's own heart (1 Samuel 13:14; Acts 13:22), whereas Saul ultimately was rejected by God for his disobedience.

David proved himself diligent in everything he put his hands to.

1 Samuel 17:16-20

> ¹⁶ *And the Philistine drew near and presented himself forty days, morning and evening.*
>
> ¹⁷ *Then Jesse said to his son David, "Take now for your brothers an ephah of this dried grain and these ten loaves and run to your brothers at the camp.*
>
> ¹⁸ *And carry these ten cheeses to the captain of their thousand, and see how your brothers fare, and bring back news of them."*
>
> ¹⁹ *Now Saul and they and all the men of Israel were in the Valley of Elah, fighting with the Philistines.*
>
> ²⁰ *So David rose early in the morning, left the sheep with a keeper, and took the things and went as Jesse had commanded him. And he came to the camp as the army was going out to the fight and shouting for the battle.*

David could have given the sheep into the care of another at any time, but still would go home to look after his father's sheep (refer to v.15). Especially after going to work for the king, David could most likely have hired a shepherd to take his place. David had the quality and character of a true son and the humility needed to be a great king.

1 Samuel 17:21-27

²¹ For Israel and the Philistines had drawn up in battle array, army against army.

²² And David left his supplies in the hand of the supply keeper, ran to the army, and came and greeted his brothers.

²³ Then as he talked with them, there was the champion, the Philistine of Gath, Goliath by name, coming up from the armies of the Philistines; and he spoke according to the same words. So David heard them.

²⁴ And all the men of Israel, when they saw the man, fled from him and were dreadfully afraid.

²⁵ So the men of Israel said, "Have you seen this man who has come up? Surely he has come up to defy Israel, and it shall be that the man who kills him the king will enrich with great riches, will give him his daughter, and give his father's house exemption from taxes in Israel."

²⁶ Then David spoke to the men who stood by him, saying, "What shall be done for the man who kills this Philistine and takes away the reproach from Israel? For who is this uncircumcised Philistine, that he should defy the armies of the living God?"

²⁷ And the people answered him in this manner, saying, "So shall it be done for the man who kills him."

As Goliath is taunting the Israelites, David is inquiring about what would happen to the man that brings down this giant.

The man that kills Goliath would receive:

- Great riches from the king.
- He would win the king's daughter in marriage (be related to the king).

- His father's house would be exempt from taxes.

This is important because it should have motivated many in Saul's army to go into action. I am sure David was confused, wondering why no one rose to the challenge, especially knowing that the one that would defeat Goliath would have been rewarded greatly. It is interesting that David never thought that the job of killing Goliath was a difficult task. He never showed any fear or apprehension of any type. Instead, he was confused as to why no one else was willing to face this giant.

1 Samuel 17:28-30

> [28] Now Eliab his oldest brother heard when he spoke to the men; and Eliab's anger was aroused against David, and he said, "Why did you come down here? And with whom have you left those few sheep in the wilderness? I know your pride and the insolence of your heart, for you have come down to see the battle."

> [29] And David said, "What have I done now? Is there not a cause?"

> [30] Then he turned from him toward another and said the same thing, and these people answered him as the first ones did.

Eliab, David's oldest brother, becomes angry at David. Eliab goes so far as to say that David is full of pride and insolence of heart. He even mocks David by asking, "And with whom have you left those few sheep in the wilderness?" I believe that Eliab was angry because his fear of Goliath was exposed by David. He showed just how emotionally weak and immature he was. Often people that are as Eliab will put down others for themselves to look and feel bigger and better than they are, just as Eliab did here with David. This is, unfortunately, the way many deal with their insecurities. They change the subject and point the finger at others; especially those who make them come face to face with their fears. Often those who are making accusations against another, as Eliab did with David, are guilty of the very accusations they are making. Many church leaders do this quite often. Problems arise and it is never their fault. They blame everyone else but themselves. Again, what are you under?

Notice David's reaction (v.29-30). David brought the conversation back to the issue at hand by saying, *"Is there not a cause?"* After the issue was at hand and in the forefront, David did what we all need to learn to do, "Then he turned from him toward another and said the same thing..." David did not remain in a conversation with someone that was verbally assaulting him. He turned and found another person to speak with. The passage does not make it clear, but I am sure David sought someone that he could talk with that was not consumed by fear and the backlash that fear creates.

1 Samuel 17:31-33

[31] *Now when the words which David spoke were heard, they reported them to Saul; and he sent for him.*

[32] *Then David said to Saul, "Let no man's heart fail because of him; your servant will go and fight with this Philistine."*

[33] *And Saul said to David, "You are not able to go against this Philistine to fight with him; for you are a youth, and he a man of war from his youth."*

Know this:

*Your words will eventually make their way
to the king (or those in authority),
just as David's words became known to Saul.*

Be aware that you will be tested in what you say. Just as Saul questioned David about the things he was saying regarding Goliath, we also will be asked regarding our claims, especially the claims of our strength and past victories.

As a church leader, I have had many people over the years try to convince me of all their exploits. One man came to my church for one service then wanted a private meeting with me. During this meeting, he told me of his credentials, the churches he served in, the people he knew, etc. For over an hour I sat and listened to this man try to sell himself to me. The whole time I sat wondering where all of this was going. After he told me everything about how great he was, he told me why I was with him in that meeting. He said, "I want to be a pastor in your church." Now, he had only been at my church for one service. I did not even know this man. As a matter of fact, I did not even know his first name. We had said hello and shook hands three days prior at church, but we were never properly introduced at that time. Here he was trying to convince me that I needed him as a pastor at my church and I did not even know his name.

When David spoke, he was not speaking of a place of seeking a title or position. He was merely wondering why no one in the king's army faced this giant. He did not go bragging about whom he was and what he had done. These things did not come up in conversation until he was before the king. David captured the attention of the right people because he was asking the right questions. These questions led him to stand before the king and explain why he could take this giant down. Unlike the man in my story, David could back up his claims with proof of his exploits and action for even greater exploits.

1 Samuel 17:34-37

34 But David said to Saul, "Your servant used to keep his father's sheep, and when a lion or a bear came and took a lamb out of the flock,

35 I went out after it and struck it, and delivered the lamb from its mouth; and when it arose against me, I caught it by its beard, and struck and killed it.

36 Your servant has killed both lion and bear; and this uncircumcised Philistine will be like one of them, seeing he has defied the armies of the living God."

37 Moreover, David said, "The LORD, who delivered me from the paw of the lion and from the paw of the bear, He will deliver me from the hand of this Philistine." And Saul said to David, "Go, and the LORD be with you!"

We must understand that we will be questioned by others when we claim that we can bring down the giants around us, so we better have some victories under our belt. We must be able to prove our achievements when questioned. I am not suggesting that we should not talk in this manner. I am only saying that we better be able to back up our claims of victory. Otherwise, we may be thrown into a battle that we are not ready for. Many have been thrown into battles that they are ill-prepared for simply because they bragged about their exploits. If you talk big in this way, then you may become engaged in a battle that you were never ready for. We must be people that act out our victories rather than speak of them only. David was someone that only brought up his victories because he was willing to face off with the giant that caused such fear in the hearts of everyone around him. He was not bragging as much as he wanted to show that he could actually bring down this giant.

This brings to mind a personal pet-peeve of mine. In the church world today many are 'title chasers'. That is a person that builds himself up by chasing after and attaching grand titles to their name. It may be the title of pastor or reverend, evangelist, apostle or prophet; the title of bishop, or my all-time favorite – revivalist! Every one of these titles should be self-evident. We are to *do* our title before we *demand* our title.

Some examples of the above:

- A pastor should be lovingly caring for and leading God's people.
- A prophet should be prophesying the mysteries of the Lord.
- A bishop should be an overseer of several churches or ministries.
- A revivalist should be a leader and steward of a revival (such as William Seymour, Kathryn Kuhlman, Smith Wigglesworth, etc.).
- An apostle should be one that goes out and establishes churches and ministries.

If we are not daily living up to the title attached to our name, we need to drop the title before we are put into a battle that we cannot win. David was a slayer of bears and lions so he could be a slayer of giants. Just as the list above proposes, those that are not living up to the title they carry should drop the title until they are doing what the title suggests. Many wear the title of the pastor, but rarely are they around the people they are to be pastoring. They come onto the platform without touching anyone or being touched by anyone; they preach their message, and then sneak out the door behind the platform. It is impossible to be a pastor without being among the people. These people should drop the title until they reevaluate what they are doing and why they do it.

1 Samuel 17:38-40

³⁸ *So Saul clothed David with his armor, and he put a bronze helmet on his head; he also clothed him with a coat of mail.*

³⁹ *David fastened his sword to his armor and tried to walk, for he had not tested them. And David said to Saul, "I cannot walk with these, for I have not tested them." So David took them off.*

⁴⁰ *Then he took his staff in his hand; and he chose for himself five smooth stones from the brook, and put them in a shepherd's bag, in a pouch which he had, and his sling was in his hand. And he drew near to the Philistine.*

David found out real fast that he could not use the armor of Saul. It was not that he would never be able to wear and use armor, but David simply could not use what he was not accustomed to. It is interesting to note that although David was anointed as king, he had not fought like a king. David still worked and functioned as a shepherd, so he had to fight dressed as a shepherd. He was not trained (nor familiar) with the attire of the king, especially on the battlefield. When we take upon ourselves the title of something we are not yet accustomed to, we will be like David in Saul's armor. We will not be able to walk or make progress as we should. The battlefield is not the place to learn how to walk in a new role (or armor). We need the safety of the training grounds to learn a new role and how to wear the armor of that role. David was a shepherd-warrior on the battlefield because he was a shepherd-warrior in the field. David could not fight as a warrior-king because he had not yet been trained as a warrior-king. This battle was about to change David forever. David was about to transition from a warrior-shepherd into a warrior-king. He was no longer going to be fighting for the sheep but for the nation.

1 Samuel 17:48

> So it was when the Philistine arose and came and drew near to meet David, that David hurried and ran toward the army to meet the Philistine.

Notice that in v. 39, David said, "*I cannot walk with these, for I have not tested them.*" His initial concern was only walking in the armor. Walking is the simplest most basic form of movement for a person (just above crawling). David would have to do more than merely walk on the battlefield. David would need to maneuver by running, jumping, crouching, etc., and in this armor, he could not even walk as he needed to.

DO NOT wear what keeps you from moving forward in the simplest and most basic of ways.

If you cannot walk and make a forward movement, you will never be able to run when you need to. It is the same in any ministry position.

Do not ever allow yourself to take a title upon yourself that you cannot maneuver in.

If you bear the title of pastor and yet are wearing armor that keeps you from running to the sheep (God's people) when the bear or lion approaches, then you will never be able to run towards the giants when the stakes are much higher.

In v. 48 we find David running towards Goliath and the battle. If he were wearing Saul's armor, he would not have been able to run into the fight, nor would he be able to maneuver on the battlefield as needed. The battlefield was not the place to train for combat or grow accustomed to new armor. The battlefield was a win or lose situation for David and all of Israel. Far too many Christians have not been able to make it onto the battlefield because they are still trying to walk in Saul's armor. Saul's armor represents past moves of God. What came before us was not bad, but when the battlefield changes, so should our tactics, weapons, and armor. It was not only true at the time of David, but it is still true for us today. The giants we are facing today are not necessarily the giants our forefathers faced.

Let Saul and his generation keep and use their armor, while this generation develops and grows in its understanding of the armor we are to wear today.

David took what he was accustomed to and what he had used to bring victory in past battles. David spoke of victories over the lion and bear, causing Saul to be at ease, but he also encouraged himself, causing him to know that this giant would be no different than the bear or lion. When it came time to fight Goliath, David used what had worked for him in the past. He used what he was accustomed to, and what he could run in.

It may seem like you are stuck with the few sheep and that you have been forgotten, but you have not! Others around you may not see much in you, as was the case with David's father and his brothers, but God is watching you. Always remember,

David may have been neglected
and kept away from the battlefield early on,
but he was the only one that was not impacted
by the fear Goliath brought.

It will be the same for many in our day and age as well. If you remain diligent to the Lord, He will raise you up, and you will bring down giants that are plaguing the region around you. Remain diligent, and you will be brought to the palace, and be the one that brings freedom to the atmosphere. Remain diligent, and God will raise you up in due season.

Chapter 11
The Veil of Obscurity

After David had defeated Goliath, some interesting things began to take place in Israel. Saul experienced a shift in the way he viewed David, and a change in the way the people of the nation saw Saul. David's victory over Goliath set in motion a chain of events that caused everything to change in Israel.

1 Samuel 18:1-5

¹ Now when he had finished speaking to Saul, the soul of Jonathan was knit to the soul of David, and Jonathan loved him as his own soul.

² Saul took him that day, and would not let him go home to his father's house anymore.

³ Then Jonathan and David made a covenant because he loved him as his own soul.

⁴ And Jonathan took off the robe that was on him and gave it to David, with his armor, even to his sword and his bow and his belt.

⁵ So David went out wherever Saul sent him and behaved wisely. And Saul set him over the men of war, and he was accepted in the sight of all the people and also in the sight of Saul's servants.

David's victory over Goliath and the victory over the Philistines that it led to, caused Saul to placed David in a very prominent place in the army of Israel. Jonathan (Saul's son) became close friends with David, and David came to permanently live in the palace. All because of his victory over the giant that caused fear in the hearts of Israel.

Keep in mind, your victories will often lead to this type of treatment from others, including those in prominent positions. The 'kings' of our day will bring the victorious around them because they want victory in their house. The leaders of successful churches and ministries will often want the best, so they will be looking for the Davids of our era to set around them. Every ministry leader will want giant slayers on their team, so they will be actively looking for and recruiting them as they are made manifest. This is what the man of understanding does. They look for the best then recruit them to work for their organization. This is a principle of those that know how to succeed in life, business, and ministry.

If you want to be the best,
surround yourself with the best.

Praise leads to a Murderous Heart

1 Samuel 18:6-9

> *[6] Now it had happened as they were coming home when David was returning from the slaughter of the Philistine, that the women had come out of all the cities of Israel, singing and dancing, to meet King Saul, with tambourines, with joy, and with musical instruments.*

[7] So the women sang as they danced, and said: "Saul has slain his thousands, And David his ten thousands."

[8] Then Saul was very angry, and the saying displeased him; and he said, "They have ascribed to David ten thousands, and to me they have ascribed only thousands. Now, what more can he have but the kingdom?"

[9] So Saul eyed David from that day forward.

What changed between David and Saul? The answer, nothing! At least in the natural. What changed was Saul's heart. Once David was given more praise than Saul, he became angry towards David. What changed was the heart of Saul when he heard people praising the victory of David over his victories.

This is something we all must be aware of. At times, when we are in the position of David, our victories will turn into proverbial celebration by those around us. During these times, we must be careful to not allow pride to grow in our hearts, but we must humble ourselves before the Lord and those around us.

Other times we will be like Saul in this story. Those that we have built up and given the position to, will at times be praised for their work more than we are being praised. At these times, we must humble ourselves before the Lord, allowing others to enjoy the limelight for the season. If we do not bring ourselves to humility, we stand to take upon ourselves the same attitude of Saul. We will become paranoid and suspicious of those around us simply because they were praised for a good work. The insecurity that plagued Saul came to the forefront when he saw that the people praised David more than him. If (or when) we ever feel this way when others are being recognized for their good work, it would do us good to remember this story.

161

It is during times of praise that the insecurities we harbor will come to the forefront of our heart and attitudes.

When we recognize these feelings and attitudes, we should take them to the Lord, humbling ourselves before we fall deeper into pride and despair.

What was it that changed in the heart of the people? The only thing that changed was that the people now could see David for who he was – a giant slayer. Once the people recognized David for who he truly was, they honored him for the man they now saw. David killed Goliath and brought freedom to the people of Israel. No longer was a hostile army on their border threatening them. Instead, the Israelites plundered the camp of the enemy because of what David did. In the natural, the only thing that changed was that David was 'exposed' as the man he truly was. The veil of obscurity was removed, and now everyone could see the man that God developed David to be: no longer merely a shepherd of sheep, but a warrior and defender of God's people.

In this story we can find several truths that will help us in life:

- People (even leaders) will want you around when you make them look good (just as David made Saul look good when he took Goliath's head).
- People are enamored by the hero (including perceived heroes, such as entertainers).
- Those in key positions will want to be your friend after a great victory.
- You will gain quick and great success after a major victory.

162

- Everyone will want to be your friend and will sing your praises when they are getting something from you.
- Often when people sing your praises louder than those over you, you will be hated by those that just days earlier loved you.

Most of these are good things, of course, but things we need to be aware of. Everyone seems to love being in this place of praise and adoration, but few recognize the obstacles and future heartache it can bring. As children, most of us wanted to be famous and adored by the world, but what many have found is that fame and praise come at a high price. Many just cannot handle the praise of others close to them. At the same time many cannot handle it when others are praised above them. We must guard our hearts for both pitfalls. Humility is the key to remaining free in both instances.

1 Samuel 18:7-9

7 So the women sang as they danced, and said: "Saul has slain his thousands, And David his ten thousands."

8 Then Saul was very angry, and the saying displeased him; and he said, "They have ascribed to David ten thousands, and to me they have ascribed only thousands. Now, what more can he have but the kingdom?"

9 So Saul eyed David from that day forward.

When the women sang of the victories of Saul and David, giving greater acclaim to David, Saul became furious at David, even though David had nothing to do with it. It was a spontaneous celebration on the part of the women in these cities, but now David was in the crosshairs of a jealous king. King Saul was eager to allow David to face the giant but had not anticipated what would happen after the victory. Saul's insecurity and weakness were exposed when the women attributed more acclamation to David. It is interesting to note that Saul, at this point, actually had more victories on the battlefield than David. David could point to killing a bear, a lion, and one giant. Saul could point to many battles against many enemies. However true, Saul was insecure to the point that he was now embittered towards David.

Saul was not secure enough within himself to allow David to receive more praise than he. Saul took this inwardly and became angry at David even though David had not solicited the acclamation from the women in these cities. This type of behavior happens more often than we may think. Leaders want to be associated with giant slayers, so they bring these Davids close to them after significant victories, only to turn on them when the praise they receive trumps the praise the leader receives. This, unfortunately, happens in the church often. A Lead Pastor will hire the 'hotshot' Youth Pastor or Worship Leader because of their great skill in ministry. Everything goes great as the church grows and moves forward until these underlings receive more praise than the pastor. Bitterness and anger are birthed in the heart of the Lead Pastor, and he begins to erode and undermine the ministries of the people that were at one time close to him. The very ones that he selected because of their skill and abilities now caused him to lose heart and plan for their demise. It is sad to know this, but most of us that have been around for a while have seen this take place.

This, of course, does not ALWAYS happen, but it happens often enough to take it seriously and guard against it. We must always be diligent to check our hearts and remove all such anger and bitterness or we will fall prey to the same deception Saul succumbed to.

Also, we must keep our hearts in check as David did. He was the object of Saul's anger and bitterness and continued to remain faithful. David was loved by Saul as long as David made Saul look good. David's victories made Saul look good as king, but he felt weakened in his position as king when David was praised more than he. This, regrettably, is a very common problem in the church as well as in business. Many reading this can identify with what I am writing. Some can identify with being the victim of such treatment, and some can identify with being the perpetrator of such treatment. In either case, we must overcome this behavior, stopping it dead in its tracks.

What if you were in Saul's position? Imagine someone under you receiving more praise from your congregation (or employees) than you. Would you be able to stay clear and free of anger and bitterness towards those that are being elevated by others' praise? Would you be able to keep that person close to your side even though more people want their autograph and picture than yours? If not, it is time for some deep repentance. If you could not continue to build up and train those that are being adored more than you, then it might be time to step away from your position at the top until your heart is right.

What if you were in David's position? Imagine being praised and adored more than those who are over you and helped you get into that position. How would you handle your new found fame? Would you shift the focus to those who helped you? Or would you eat up the attention, ignoring those over you as though they were now insignificant?

These questions are imperative for us to ponder, because at times we will be in the position such as David, and at other times we will be in the position of Saul. How we handle these situations will expose who we really are. Our heart and character will be on display before God and the world around us. It would do us all well to search our own hearts and make the needed adjustments long before we are thrust into one of these situations. Once in the situation, it is often too late to train or retrain our heart towards righteousness. If we do not make the needed changes before we come into this situation, it may be too late. Our words and actions will have already been set in the hearts and minds of those around us for good or for evil.

1 Samuel 18:11

> And Saul cast the spear, for he said, "I will pin David to the wall!" But David escaped his presence twice.

When people start singing your praises, **be careful**! Some will become very jealous of your success and will try to 'pin (you) to the wall'! As one group is shouting their love for you, another group will be conspiring against you. It is a terrible thing but nonetheless true. This is not to be fearful of everyone around you, but to be sober-minded and aware of what is going on, so that you are not caught off guard when these things arise. Some will stand with you through thick and thin, but others will be jealous and angry with you when you succeed.

Most often those who become jealous
of another's success are those that helped train
and develop the very ones that are now
growing in popularity.

Each move of God is criticized most
by those in the previous move of God.

It is a strange thing to witness, and yet is true. It is hard to admit this, but our greatest critics are often our spiritual fathers and mothers – the ones that helped us succeed and achieve the victories that have brought the praises and adoration of others. This has been true in my life, and the lives of many others. Those that should be rejoicing with us in our victories often become our greatest critics. Jealousy is an ugly thing.

If we are to be healthy and whole as a church, we need to overcome these issues once and for all. The mature saints must not act like Saul, but instead behave like spiritual fathers and mothers. Instead of jealousy, anger, and bitterness, we need to express joy, love, and excitement when our spiritual children do more than we have done. We must keep in mind that the Davids among us would never be in the position they are in without our help. They are slaying giants because of our input and training.

As spiritual parents,
we are to be overwhelmed with joy when our
sons and daughters in the faith are bringing
down giants, taking territory and
experiencing significant victories.

At the same time, those receiving the praises and adoration of those around them need to be humble enough to divert that praise to God and to those He put in their lives to develop them. We did not get to that place of adoration on our own. We need to show our deep appreciation for those who have been as fathers and mothers in the faith to us.

David could have saved himself a world of hurt had he praised Saul openly the moment he heard the women preferring him over Saul. I know that hindsight is 20/20, but we can learn some powerful lessons about honor from this story.

Many years ago, I was the associate pastor of the church I attended. The lead apostle was the overseer of two churches about an hour's drive from one another. This apostle had told my wife and me that he wanted us to become the lead pastor of the church we attended. For several years we worked hard in the church under the idea that soon we would take the reins fully of that church. Out of the blue, the apostle turned the church over to the head deacon of the church, right out from under me. No communication occurred before this happened, nor afterward. To this day, I have no idea why I was lied to and led on in such a manner, but being openly humiliated in this church was one of the best things that ever happened to me.

This caused me to reevaluate why I was in that church. It made me reevaluate my relationship with this man and those like him. I learned what not to do in ministry, and that has had a greater impact on me than all the 'how-to' lists. Like David, I learned much from this Saul as well. I watched him and learned how to treat people and how not to treat people. This may sound strange, but the Sauls of the world have a great deal to teach us, even if it is what *not* to do.

Chapter 12
It is Time for a Revolution

The Questions We Must Ask

David had prevailed over Goliath, the Philistine champion, the one that taunted God and the armies of Israel. David took him down with a stone from a slingshot, removing Goliath's head with his own sword. Not only did David free Israel from the taunts and oppression of this wicked giant, but did it in such a way that the rest of the Philistines ran in fear of losing their lives. Whether David meant it or not, his victory over Goliath was done in a manner that put God's delivering power on magnificent display before everyone at the scene. The extravagant way David took down Goliath and removed his head caused a radical change in the hearts of everyone present. To the Israelites it meant strength and courage replacing fear and anxiety of heart; to the Philistines, it meant the destruction of the arrogance and haughtiness of heart being replaced with terror and dread as they ran for their lives. David's courage changed everything and everyone around him.

This is one of the greatest reasons we are in transition right now. We (the church) have been taunted and mocked by the giants of the day. All around us have been those that have thrown insults and heckled the church for years in a similar manner as Goliath.

God is now rising up the modern day Davids
that will have the wisdom and courage to face
these giants on the philosophical and ideological
battlefields of our day and age.

These Davids will not merely have the courage to step onto the battlefield, but will have the wisdom and knowledge to win the debates of the day, thus winning the hearts and minds of those watching and listening to this battle of concepts and ideas. These Davids will not merely win arguments and debates, but will have the ability to supernaturally remove the head of these giants intellectually, philosophically, and ideologically. When this takes place even the followers of the giants (modern Philistines) will turn to the One True God because of the anointed wisdom, revelation, and knowledge of the Davids that run to the battlefield.

Many look at the world today, our cultures and society, and think the problem is too big for a David to arise and fix. Many would even say that it is hopeless because it would take tens of thousands of Davids in every sphere of society and culture worldwide to even begin to turn things around. To this I would answer: You are absolutely correct! The problem truly is too big for even a handful of Davids to turn around, but do not underestimate the ripple-effect of a single warrior on the battlefield. David was more than a warrior and deliverer. He was a catalyst, a seed planted that would reproduce itself and bring in a great harvest.

¹⁵ *When the Philistines were at war again with Israel, David and his servants with him went down and fought against the Philistines; and David grew faint.*

¹⁶ *Then Ishbi-Benob, who was one of the sons of the giant, the weight of whose bronze spear was three hundred shekels, who was bearing a new sword, thought he could kill David.*

¹⁷ *But Abishai the son of Zeruiah came to his aid, and struck the Philistine and killed him. Then the men of David swore to him, saying, "You shall go out no more with us to battle, lest you quench the lamp of Israel."*

¹⁸ *Now it happened afterward that there was again a battle with the Philistines at Gob. Then Sibbechai the Hushathite killed Saph, who was one of the sons of the giant.*

¹⁹ *Again there was war at Gob with the Philistines, where Elhanan the son of Jaare-Oregim the Bethlehemite killed the brother of Goliath the Gittite, the shaft of whose spear was like a weaver's beam.*

²⁰ *Yet again there was war at Gath, where there was a man of great stature, who had six fingers on each hand and six toes on each foot, twenty-four in number; and he also was born to the giant.*

²¹ *So when he defied Israel, Jonathan the son of Shimea, David's brother, killed him.*

²² *These four were born to the giant in Gath, and fell by the hand of David and by the hand of his servants.*

You Are Contagious

It is worth noting that each and every one of us is contagious. People are catching something from you, whether good or bad. This needs to be understood in the church today. The real questions now are: "What are people catching from you? What are people catching from us?" It is not a question of whether others are catching something from us, but *what* they are catching. Think about this for a moment. Are you spreading fear, discouragement, discord, anger, etc., or are you spreading peace, joy, courage, strength, etc.? It is not a question of "if" you are contagious; it is a question of, "What you are spreading;" "What are people catching from you?" Just as communicable diseases can affect us physically, what is in our hearts and souls is equally transmissible as well. Strength and courage, along with fear and doubt can be just as infectious as the common cold or flu.

David's giant-killing courage was so contagious that even those who would make up his 'mighty men' became giant killers. Those that were around David caught what David was infused with – courage! Just one giant brought fear to all of Israel, but now killing giants seemed almost commonplace. David's courage had rubbed off on those around him. King Saul was afraid, so all under his command became afraid as well. Now everyone under David's leadership had courage and strength of heart, some becoming giant killers as David was. This is a principle that we all must understand.

Those around us (especially those under our care) will catch what we are infected with. Be it positive or negative, people will be infected with what we have.

I want to revisit something I touched upon previously.

You MUST understand that what you are under will eventually manifest in you.

The church you attend and leadership you are under (the pastor and his preaching, worship leader, youth pastor, elders, etc.) is shaping you into the image of the one that you are subject to, more than you know. This is a principle that cannot be changed or avoided. If you are hearing sermons that are founded in fear, anger, greed, lasciviousness, etc. this is what you are becoming. These words are shaping you, and you most likely do not realize it.

If you are in a church filled with faith, strength, courage, peace, joy, etc. that is what you are becoming.

What you subject yourself to is what you will become.

I know people that attend churches that major on end-time theology (eschatology) because the church leadership is fearful of world events. Without fail, if these people remain as active members of these churches for very long, they all will have a foundation of fear established within them. I know some that have become so fearful that they are afraid to travel away from home out of fear that something catastrophic could happen and they would be cut off from home and their loved ones. I personally know people that used to go on short term missions trips but are no longer willing to go because of the fear I just described. They are now too afraid to go minister away from home, because they think the antichrist may come on the scene and keep them from getting home. They became what they subjected themselves to — they are now fearful, hopeless, and powerless because this is what they submitted themselves to week after week.

The "Word of Faith" movement was a movement that revealed the hearts of many in the body of Christ. The basis of the movement and its principles were correct and much-needed in the church, but what many made of it was repulsive. Many that adhered to the principles of the Word of Faith movement did so for entirely self-centered reasons, twisting the faith principles for bigger churches, bigger houses, nicer clothes, and expensive cars. None of these things are bad, but when that is all some have to expend their faith on, it shows that not only was their theology twisted, but that it came from twisted hearts as well.

What was given by God to increase faith
for souls and to change entire regions became
a pseudo-faith for luxuries.

What should have been used to change to world
often was used to line pocketbooks.

This is not to say that the foundational principles of the Word of Faith movement are wrong, nor is it to say that everyone in of the Word of Faith camp was wrong. I am merely pointing out several of the excesses by some of those who attached themselves to this restorative move of God. It is a sad reality, but in every move of God these types of things happen. Unfortunately some will pervert the truth for their own gain and for their own self-exalting carnality. We cannot dismiss an entire move of God simply because of those that pervert the truth, but it does make it difficult to defend the movement when these extremes are raised up and viewed as the norm.

I had a discussion with a self-proclaimed man of faith once that revealed where his heart was. I said to him, "Where you and the other Word of Faith ministers went wrong was you had faith for bigger houses, bigger cars, and nicer clothes, but you let your generation go to hell because you did not have faith for them." To this he struggled with his thoughts as he mumbled something incoherently, then he sighed and said, "You are absolutely correct. We were too busy excising our faith for things, that we forgot souls." In this conversation, I was not trying to embarrass this man or humiliate him in any way. Instead, I merely wanted to point out something that needed to be rectified. I wanted him to know that it was correct to have faith and use his faith, but it needed to be adjusted to the more important things, such as the people Jesus died for.

Remember, you will become what you are under. Each of the people under this man's ministry was receiving from this type of twisted perversion of truth each time they sat under him and his teaching. Each member of his church was becoming someone that would use right principles for selfish gain. This is not an assumption, but it is a fact. If you sit in the sun you get sunburned; if you sit in the rain, you get wet. Basic but nonetheless true.

If you continue under erroneous theology,
you will have a wrong understanding of God
and His principles.

I wish I had the ability to open up every believer's heart and soul and pour this truth in.

You will become what you subject yourself to!

Of course, no one is perfect in all their theology, but the Bible is very clear about these things.

Luke 6:45

> *A good man out of the good treasure of his heart brings forth good, and an evil man out of the evil treasure of his heart brings forth evil. For out of the abundance of the heart, his mouth speaks.*

You can get a pretty good idea of what is in a preacher's heart by what he or she preaches. One sermon will not necessarily show what is in his heart, but over the course of three to six months a great deal of who a person truly is can be recognized by what is being said from the pulpit week each week. A person's true nature cannot be hidden for long, especially when they are speaking so much. A genuine essence of who they are will be exposed over time. We in the body of Christ must begin to be very honest with ourselves about this reality. Often, we will allow ourselves to be shaped by the carnality and negativity of others simply because we are self-deluded and dishonest with ourselves about what we are giving ourselves to. It is past time to take an honest look at ourselves and the teaching we have been subjecting ourselves to.

I write this next section not to cause problems, but to expose behavior that can be repaired if hearts are right. Often we engage in behavior that is wrong without knowing that it is wrong. This is usually because it is learned behavior. Regarding church leadership, we learn from our spiritual fathers and those who are mentoring us in the ministry. Most of the time what we learn from others is fantastic and will be of great benefit to ourselves and the people we minister to. Then sometimes we learn things that only miss the mark and do not measure up to the way God would have us minister. Below are a few examples:

- If you are in a church that takes more than one offering in a service, the leadership is most likely motivated by greed, lust, and power.
- If you are made to feel guilty for not giving more in the offering, the pastor is probably driven by greed, as well as by a controlling and manipulative spirit.
- If the pastor is treated like a king with several armor bearers around him, you are in a church led by someone that is most likely arrogant, self-centered, and self-exalting.
- If the pastor sits on the platform in a throne-like chair and rarely moves during praise and worship, you are in a church led by someone that is most likely pompous, haughty, arrogant, and self-exalting.

However, if you are in a church where the pastor sits on the same type of chair as anyone else, is not moved by the offering, praises and worships God along with everyone else, and serves the congregation by waiting on them, then you are under someone most likely with a heart after God and a heart for the people he was entrusted with.

If you are under greedy leadership, you are becoming greedy yourself. If you are under manipulative and self-centered leadership, you are becoming manipulative and self-centered as well.

177

What you are under, you are becoming.

This is an inescapable principle. If you are under leadership that has a pure heart for God and the people God has entrusted to him, then you are becoming individuals with a heart after God and those He loves. You are becoming what you are under.

We MUST grow up in righteousness and the proper way we are to function as a church and the house of God. It is not merely the job of the pastor to make sure that the church is operating as it should, but it is up to everyone to make sure that the things being taught are correct. All of us, regardless of our title, are supposed to search the scriptures to make sure that what we are being taught is Biblically sound.

Acts 17:11

> *These were more fair-minded than those in Thessalonica, in that they received the word with all readiness, and searched the Scriptures daily to find out whether these things were so.*

This verse shows us that it is not the job of the preacher only to search the scriptures. It is a requirement of us all to search the scriptures, so that we will know if what we are hearing is Biblically correct or if it is askew. We will never fully know if what we are being taught is actually the truth or a perversion of truth until we study it for ourselves. If more Christians took this approach, I am of the opinion that many churches would be in serious trouble. Many preachers would be faced with angry parishioners demanding they preach and teach the truth or else someone is going to be leaving — them or the pastor. However, in the long run, it would mean greater health and wholeness in the body of Christ because every preacher would know that their message better be theologically correct because they are being watched. They will be aware that the congregation will not tolerate false or weak doctrine. They will be mindful of the fact that they will have to preach and teach the truth that empowers their congregations to do great things. A revolution is coming to the church and it is beginning with those who search the word of God.

Mark 10:45

For even the Son of Man did not come to be served, but to serve, and to give His life a ransom for many."

If today's church understood this one verse and the principle found in it, many pastors and preachers would be in big trouble. Church boards would be actively looking for a new pastor to come lead their church. They would be looking for pastors that had the heart of a pastor, not merely the title of one. I, for one, believe we are past due for a revolution in this area. The church has neglected its duty in this realm for too long and as a result, many bad seeds have been sown because of it. We MUST wake up and get the House of God in order – His order!

It is time pastors and church leaders become interested in the overall spiritual health of the people God has entrusted to them, more so than their own personal pleasure and self-importance birthed from carnality of heart. A true humility needs to sweep through the church, causing us to be more concerned about the well-being of those around us than the suits we wear and the cars we drive. I am looking for the day when pastors and church leaders are once again seen in the soup lines, not looking for a bowl of soup, but serving the bowl of soup to others. I am looking for the day when once again pastors and church leadership spend more time with the people of their church than they do in the green room being waited upon. I am waiting for the hearts and minds of church leaders to be turned more towards others and what they can give, than to themselves and what they can receive. It is time for a revolution!

It is interesting to note that David did not realize the firestorm that he would cause when he brought down Goliath. This one victory caused Saul to hate him, the people to praise him, his enemies to fear him, and a new order of giant killers to arise. David did not go looking for these things; he was merely obedient to his father. His submissive heart put him in the right place at the right time. His faithfulness set things into motion that changed the course of the entire nation. You are worthy of such victories. David is not so unique that you could not do what he did. You have had victories over those things that may seem small and insignificant, but it has opened the way for greater achievements. Be obedient and faithful to the call on your life. Stay the course, and in due season you will have others praising you and singing of your victory over the giant of the day. When that happens, get ready for everything around you to change.

I want to ask you this question again, "What are people catching from you?" You are contagious whether you realize it or not, but what exactly are people catching from you? As we can plainly see with David, people caught his courage in the face of considerable opposition and danger. Saul caught freedom of heart and mind when David played and sang. The people caught a great king because he was first a great shepherd.

What are people catching from you?

Be honest with yourself and with God as you answer this. Keep in mind that Saul was removed partially because the people were catching fear, disobedience, anger, and the like from him. David was exalted because he was a man after God's own heart, and the people were catching that.

Chapter 13
Who Do You Identify With?

What I have tried to convey in this book is that we are in the process of a significant change in the world and its systems, as well as in the church worldwide. Everything is changing, and everything is rearranging. Those who are aware of the changes and are prepared for them will succeed and increase substantially.

Those who are unaware of the changes –
what they mean and why these changes are
taking place – will fall far behind and are close
to becoming incredibly irrelevant.

Worse yet, those that fight against the changes will invariably fall so far behind that they will be found fighting against God Himself. We must be people that have our eyes, ears, and hearts open to all that God is doing, being found working with Him to accomplish His purposes. Unfortunately, most are still unaware of the changes God is bringing or are fighting against these changes as if their opposition actually counted for anything other than the irritating buzzing of a mosquito.

It is a sad truth, but when we are found fighting
against God's will, we have relegated ourselves
to nothing more than a buzzing in His ears,

an irritating pest that gets brushed away,
or swatted.

Each and every believer should be able to identify themselves with someone written about in this book. If not, it is not because of the lack of content in these pages, but the lack of honesty in one's heart. That is not so much a judgment call as it is simply a fact that we must contend with, as it takes complete honesty with oneself to know fully which character we identify with and why. Until we are honest enough to face the truth about our present condition, we will never be able to make the needed changes that will transform us into one that can function in what God is doing now.

We will continue to grow more and more irrelevant and move further away from the center of God's will for us as He brings an encompassing shift into the world around us. I do not know about you, but I for one want to be a relevant part of God's work and purpose in the earth today, tomorrow, and into eternity. I do not merely want to make an impact on my generation, but I want to influence generations that have not been born yet. This will not happen if we become and remain stuck in the things the culture of today demands. We all will be significant and will make a lasting impact when we become locked into the culture of God, which is an ever-changing, and an ever-growing culture. God's culture is never stuck, but is always moving forward and growing.

Who do you identify with?

Do You Identify With David?

Everyone wants to identify with David, because after all, he was a man after God's heart (1 Samuel 13:14; Acts 13:22). This is what everyone wants to claim, but few actually fit this category and description. Many pretend to be as David was, a man or woman after God's heart, but by making this claim of ourselves proves otherwise. It was God that said David was a man after His own heart. David did not say this about himself; God said this about David. As long as we are making these statements over ourselves, it is proof of a self-exalting pride that disqualifies us from being a man or woman after God's heart. As harsh as this may sound it is still true.

This is not to say that you cannot identify with other aspects of David, his life and ministry. You can absolutely identify with some aspect of David's life, such as when he was a shepherd boy, forgotten about when it came to the banquet that would establish the next king of Israel. It could be that you identified with David when he was running from a murderous Saul that was bent on his destruction. Identifying with these aspects of David's life does not necessarily point to pride and self-exaltation, but our hearts still need to be scrutinized before we allow these identifying markers to convince us that we are more than we actually are at this present time.

We must learn to allow the Holy Spirit to bring about the changes needed so that we can grow from one on the run from the king we once served, to a king that has a heart after God.

This type of change and transformation is a work of the Holy Spirit on the inside, not a work of the flesh on the outside.

If you were to honestly and openly answer the question as to which of these characters you identify most with, which one would you say? Remember, it takes great honesty of heart towards oneself to answer that question with any real truth. God knows exactly who you are, who you most look like and what your answer would be when asked this question. Would your answer about who you identify with match God's answer if He was asked the same question about you? To say we must be honest to God in this regard is to completely miss the point. God already knows who you are and what you are all about. We need to learn to be completely and brutally honest with ourselves. Only in this way can we get an accurate picture of who we are without the fear of being rebuked by God.

Is it Eli?

Many all around us are very much like Eli. When our focus was on Eli, some things stood out about him and his leadership that is recognized in many of today's leaders. He remained in his position as High Priest long after he disqualified himself for that position. Eli was blind and had grown fat to the point that his size and weight was a major factor in his death. Both of these attributes disqualified Eli from properly performing his duties as a High Priest, but he refused to remove himself from this role. He looked to a little boy named Samuel to minister before the Lord on his behalf.

Not only was Eli disqualified because of his physical limitations (limitations he brought upon himself), but he also

186

disqualified himself because of the way he raised his sons, Hophni and Phinehas. It was not merely that his sons turned out to be corrupt, but Eli kept them both in the priesthood even after God had warned him about his sons and their wickedness. Eli's feeble parenting skills affected the entire nation, for the wickedness of Hophni and Phinehas was seen and felt by everyone that came to worship in Shiloh.

It is unfortunate, but many in leadership today cannot seem to understand just how bad it is when their children and family are out of order. You must understand that...

How a leader raises his children is an indication of how he will raise up those in his care in other places, such as a church or ministry.

To put it bluntly, if a man cannot pastor and lead his family then he cannot lead a church.

When writing about church leadership (bishops), Paul says this:

1 Timothy 3:4-5

4 *one who rules his own house well, having his children in submission with all reverence*

5 *(for if a man does not know how to rule his own house, how will he take care of the church of God?)*

What does your home look like? Are your children respectful? Do they honor you and those around them? Do they honor and serve God? If not, then the reality is you look more like Eli than you may want to admit. Your family is your first congregation. You should not try to lead a second congregation until you effectively and successfully lead and pastor your first congregation – the congregation in your home. If every pastor and church leader in the body of Christ took this seriously, the church and the world would look much more holy and righteous than it does at this present time.

While reading this, maybe you feel that you identify more with Hophni and Phinehas. Perhaps you know that you are lacking in some areas spiritually and struggle with sin, moral failures, and short-comings. You may even know that much of it can be traced back to the way you were raised, especially by your spiritual mothers and fathers. If this is the case, then it is time to reach out to someone that is mature and will spend time with you, teaching and training you properly for ministry and for life in general.

Early on in my ministry, I would cry out to God to bring older saints into my life to teach and train me. I knew that I lacked wisdom and understanding, the type that comes only with age or by a supernatural impartation of the Spirit. I made so many mistakes that I knew could have been avoided if only I had a true father in the Spirit to raise me up and share with me the wisdom he had. I can honestly say that God has blessed me over the years with several father figures that poured themselves into me. The wisdom and understanding that took them years to develop were being shared and given to me through their instruction and impartation.

At times these spiritual fathers corrected and rebuked me, teaching me that I could not get away with turning a blind eye to my failures and sin. They showed me that I had to deal with it and overcome it before I continued as I wanted. These men did not want me to be their Hophni or Phinehas, but instead be their

Samuel or David. I am so grateful for the words of wisdom, the training, and even the correction that I received because it helped me to become a leader that can successfully lead both my family and the congregation God has entrusted to me.

Samuel was a little boy when he was brought to live in the tabernacle under Eli's care. He was brought to the most prominent location and place of Israel's worship at a time when the fate of the nation was in the balance. This little boy named Samuel was being raised by the man that failed his own sons, was disobedient to God, and was weakening the nation. It seemed impossible for Samuel to become a man that could bring restoration to the land, but God had a plan. It was through Samuel that God would restore the prophetic word of the Lord to His people. Samuel restored what Eli and his sons had destroyed. Many in the body of Christ today are like Samuel. They are being raised up in the house of Eli, but will soon be revealed for who they are before God. These Samuels will bring a much needed restoration to the body of Christ.

Is it Samuel?

Is it Samuel you most identify with? For all intents and purposes, Samuel was abandoned by his father and mother and left at the tabernacle to be raised by a stranger. Samuel was expected to do the job that Eli could no longer do because of his failing health and his refusal to step down from his position as High Priest. This little boy was under a great deal of pressure: pressure to repair what the present priesthood had corrupted and destroyed. The restoration was coming through a little boy that had been given up by his parents and raised by a corrupt priest in the house of worship of Israel.

Some reading this feel as if they are like Samuel. You feel that if it were not for you, the whole church and ministry would fall apart. You may not get the recognition that you feel you deserve, but your feeling is that if you were to leave or step down, the church would greatly suffer because of the present leadership. You are concerned that the Elis around you would destroy everything you have worked so hard to build up. Do not forget that Samuel had to be trained for several years before he was recognized as anything more than the one that served Eli in the tabernacle. Samuel was no more than a servant of the High Priest until God said otherwise. It is the same with all who identify with Samuel. God will unveil you to the church and those around you when your training is complete and the time is up for those you are to replace. As hard as it might seem at times, do not get ahead of the process. God knows what He is doing, and He will reveal you and His plan for you when the time is right.

Is it Saul?

Perhaps you identify most with King Saul. You know you have been chosen by God because of your apparent God-given abilities, and you know that you have what it takes to be a great leader, but you are always struggling with your self-image, hiding among the baggage when you should be standing head and shoulders above the competition. Many in the body of Christ today can be looked upon as a modern Saul. Keep in mind Saul was God's first pick. Man did not choose Saul, God chose Saul.

It is not bad to be as King Saul was, at least in the beginning of his reign. Saul begins to fail as a king because he neglected to first deal with the inner struggle of his self-image. It was not until David received more praise from the people than Saul received that the weakness of his heart was fully exposed. It was at that point that Saul's heart condition was on full display. He had already set things in motion when he failed to do all that God had commanded him. This led to his anger toward David. Saul's insecurity led him to try to destroy David.

Before the people praised David for his accomplishments, Saul loved David like he was his son, but now he sought to kill him for one reason and one reason only. In Saul's mind, the people loved and appreciated David more than they loved him. Saul was insecure within himself because of his low self-image, so much so, that murder was conceived in his heart. Once conceived, he gave into the fear, anger, and bitterness that was birthed in his heart, and tried to kill David.

It is unfortunate, but this is a problem with many leaders in the body of Christ today. They cannot stand the idea that someone else in their church or organization could be loved, honored or praised more than they are. When they hear of others receiving recognition from the people, they get angry or bitter (or both), and they begin to attack these ones as Saul attacked David. Oh, do not get me wrong - I am not saying physical spears are being thrown in the church. However, you will see spears of lies, spears of accusation, spears of disrespect, spears of insults, and spears of dissension thrown by weak leaders every day. Who are they throwing these spears at? Those who faithfully serve them. Those that serve the church but receive recognition from the people around them to a greater degree than what the leaders receive themselves. These are the Davids that the modern-day Sauls are seeking to kill.

As I was writing this several persons came to mind. People that are truly modern day Sauls. They operate from hearts of insecurity that is not recognizable until someone else is praised for their accomplishments more than they are. When someone else is given the spotlight, the seeds of murder are sown in the hearts of these Sauls. It is not long before the spears are being thrown at the Davids in an attempt to discredit and bring down the one they felt robbed them of their glory.

It is sad, but each of us could put names and faces to this. Every one of us has seen or experienced this in some way. Unfortunately we have more Sauls in the church today than we want to admit.

This again is where we need to be truly honest with ourselves. If this is you, and if this is something that you struggle with, you need to be honest with yourself and God and seek to have your heart strengthened and healed before you fall as Saul did. Remember...

Saul had everything that he needed
to be a great king and a great leader.

You have everything you need
to be a great leader among God's people.

However, we can all fail as Saul did if we do not deal with the issues of our hearts. When we realize we struggle with these types of issues, we need to seek deliverance and healing in our hearts so that we do not fail and have the same end as Saul. If

God called you – indeed called you, and He opened the door and placed you in a leadership position, then He has also given you access to absolutely everything you need to overcome every issue of the heart that would cause you to stumble and fail as a leader. The only way that you and I can fail as leaders is if we neglect to take hold of what God has already given us. One of the first things He has given us access to is strength of heart, strength of mind, and strength of spirit.

Philippians 2:13
...for it is God who works in you both to will and to do for His good pleasure.

Yet, just because we have access to these things does not mean we automatically take advantage of these things. They are freely given to us by God, but we must take hold of them and apply them to our life and use them.

To everyone reading this that can honestly say they identify with King Saul, it is my hope and my prayer that you do not just stop with that realization, but you go on to seek and receive the healing and the strength of heart that God has for you. You do not need to end the way Saul did.

You may identify with Saul right now, but your end could be much different than Saul's. You can take advantage of those around you that have healing in their hands and a word of deliverance in their mouth. You can receive what you need to become the leader that God wants you to become. Keep in mind Saul first had Samuel, a great prophet, at his disposal, but he did not seek him for the right things at the right time. Saul also had David who could play the harp and drive evil spirits away, but he did not take it a step further by repenting and seeking genuine forgiveness and healing of the heart. Instead, he used David for momentary clarity of thinking, instead of using that same delivering power that was in David's harp for long-term, long-lasting deliverance and freedom of spirit. No one in the body of Christ needs to end their life and ministry in tragedy as did Saul. Each of us has been given access to healing and deliverance of heart and mind so that we can end strong and well.

Romans 12:2

> *And do not be conformed to this world, but be transformed by the renewing of your mind, that you may prove what is that good and acceptable and perfect will of God.*

Know Who You Are

No matter where you are in your spiritual development, you will always have more to achieve. You may find yourself identifying with one of the less savory characters in this book, but we always can find room for growth. It is not where you are presently that is the problem. The problems begin when you are unwilling to change. "Renewing of your mind" begins with doing things differently than you have done them before. You may have sought counsel in the past, so do it again but seek it from someone that you know will tell you the truth and hold you accountable. Do not give up the pursuit of perfection (James 1:4), but press on into the fullness of what God has for you.

Ephesians 4:22-24

> [22] *that you put off, concerning your former conduct, the old man which grows corrupt according to the deceitful lusts,*

23 and be renewed in the spirit of your mind,

24 and that you put on the new man which was created according to God, in true righteousness and holiness.

If you are willing to "put off...the old man" and "put on the new man," you will grow and achieve great things. No one needs to stay where they are at this present time. The person you identify with now does not have to be the person you identify with a year from now. God has new things in store for the one that is willing to put off the old and embrace the new. The new man is the true you that has been created in the likeness of Jesus. Do not settle for lesser things or a lower existence.

> **The new man is created in a manner that looks like God, for God is the model for the new man.**

In other words, we have not only been given access to God and His character and nature, but we have been made to look like Him. Come up to the real you.

It is unfortunate, but many Christians simply do not walk out (or live according to) who they really are. As a matter of fact, we all struggle in this area. It is my desire – my life goal, to come to the place where I live from the fullness of my faith and relationship with Jesus, but also rise up a generation that will do the same

I will have failed in my earthly mission if I and those I teach never fully attain to what has been promised us and spoken to us in the words of Scripture.

The disciples of Jesus had similar problems with their identity. After being with Jesus, hearing Him preach and teach, seeing the miracles and healings, they still struggled with His identity, which caused them to struggle with their own. Seeing that they struggled at times with who Jesus was, they struggled with who they were as well.

> *It is a fact that those who struggle with*
> *the identity of Jesus will always struggle*
> *with their own identity.*

Who we truly are before God goes far beyond the characters written about in this book. However, you will see many overlapping characteristics between you and at least one character in this book.

The battle over your identity is the most important battle you will fight. It is tied directly to the identity of Jesus. If you do not know who <u>He</u> is, you will never know who <u>you</u> are. If you do not know who <u>you</u> are, you will never know who <u>He</u> is. Your identity and His are tied together. This is because the Bible teaches that Christ is in you and that you are in Christ. Your relationship with Jesus is far greater and deeper than any other relationship you will ever have. If you struggle in your relationship with Christ, you will also struggle to clearly understand who you are, and are to be.

It should be the aim of us all to not only identify with Jesus, but to be like Him. Being Christ-like is what we aspire to. You might identify with one of the other characters in this book at this stage of your life, but continue to grow in the things of the LORD and you will take on the image of Christ (Rom 8:29).

The Bible tells us that Jesus is Our Lord and Savior (2 Pet 2:20). These two characteristics belong to Jesus alone; however, there are many attributes of Jesus that we can take upon ourselves.

Jesus is the Chosen One and an Indescribable Gift (Luke 23:35; 2 Cor 9:15); He is an Intercessor and Mediator (Heb 7:25; 1 Tim 2:5); a friend of tax collectors and sinners (Matt 11:19). Scripture also describes Jesus as a Good Shepherd (John 10:11, 14), a Holy Servant (Acts 4:27) and the Image of God (2 Cor 4:4; Col 1:15). You will find that Jesus is the Light of the World (John 8:12), and He tells us that we are the Light of the World (Matt 5:14).

This is merely a small portion of what could be written about Jesus. There isn't room enough to write about everything that set Jesus apart from others. He is the ultimate standard of our faith and life. Many would say, "I could never measure up to Christ." And yet we are commanded to "put on Christ" (Rom 13:14). We would not find this command if it were not possible. So, the question remains: Do you identify with Jesus?

> ### *Knowing Christ means that you will also know who you are.*

Satan does not want us to know our true identity. He will do everything he can to cause us to question who we are and what we are to be. If he is successful at getting us to question what God has said about us (our identity), we will not fulfill the call of God on our life because we will never fully know who we are.

> ### *One of Satan's tactics is to keep us from honestly assessing who we identify with.*

As I wrote earlier, we all want to be like Samuel or David. No one intends to identify with Saul, Eli or his corrupt children.

However, if we are associated with these but we have been blinded to this truth, we will never be able to grow beyond this level of identity. If Satan can convince you that you are a Samuel when in reality you are an Eli, you will never be able to grow into a Samuel until you can see this clearly and honestly. You will never face the truth of who you are as long as you allow the enemy to put his veil over your eyes.

The issues we face in life and with our identity God has more than compensated for through the cross and sacrificial death of Jesus. With the death, burial and resurrection of Jesus, we have been saved, and given a new nature. This new nature is far more than a mere mindset or attitude; it is a full restoration back to God and His original design for us. In this case, our identity is not merely who we are at the moment, but who we truly are, the reason why we have been created.

Identity not only tells us who we are,
but what we are and how we are to live
and exist, as well as what we are capable of.

Knowing your identity is the first step
to becoming the person you were created to be.

Satan wants to keep us from becoming everything God wants us to become. He is frightened at the destruction that you will cause his kingdom if you ever fully understand exactly who you are. When you know what you have been created for and you become that, you will be empowered in such a way that brings destruction to the enemy. For this reason, you have become a target for the enemy, as he will do all that he can to keep you from becoming all that you were created to be. One of the best ways to overcome the lies of the enemy is to be honest with yourself about who and what you are right now so that you can make the needed adjustments to grow into the person God created you to be.

Each of us is to be as David was: "a man after God's own heart." Each of us is to grow into a leader that is intimate with our Father, and that can be used to restore the kingdom around us. We are also to be like Samuel: one that is restoring the prophetic Word of the Lord that brings breakthrough. We are to rise up in power and restore all that was lost and destroyed by those who were corrupt. Our true identity is that of a restorer of righteousness and the power of God.

Each of us is of great value to God, His kingdom, and the restoration of all things (Acts 3:19-21). Until we can identify ourselves for who and what we presently are, and identify ourselves with who and what we are to become, we will never fulfill God's plans and purposes for our lives. When we know who we are, and where we are going, we can work with God to become all that we are to be. The world needs us to become what God has called us to be. Allow God to bring you through the needed transitions and changes so that you will rise to the level that God has established for you. It is time for a change, it is time for a revolution, and it is time for transition.